Sniffy™
THE VIRTUAL RAT
Lite Version 2.0

Tom Alloway
University of Toronto at Mississauga

Greg Wilson
DID Software

Jeff Graham
University of Toronto at Mississauga

WADSWORTH
CENGAGE Learning™

Australia • Brazil • Japan • Korea • Mexico • Singapore • Spain • United Kingdom • United States

WADSWORTH
CENGAGE Learning

Sniffy the Virtual Rat: Lite Version 2.0
Tom Alloway, Greg Wilson, Jeff Graham

Psychology Editor: Marianne Taflinger

Assistant Editor: Jennifer Keever

Editorial Assistant: Justin Courts

Technology Project Manager: Darin Derstine

Marketing Manager: Chris Caldeira

Marketing Assistant: Laurel Anderson

Advertising Project Manager: Brian Chaffee

Art Director: Vernon Boes

Print/Media Buyer: Lisa Claudeanos

Permissions Editor: Audrey Pettengill

Production Service/Compositor: Scratchgravel Publishing Services

Copy Editor: Toni Z. Ackley

Cover Designer: Katherine Minerva

Cover Image: Integrated Circuits © Lester Lefkowitz/CORBIS, White Mouse, Getty Images, Inc.

Trademark Notice
Apple, the Apple logo, AppleLink, AppleShare, QuickTime, ResEdit, PowerPC, and Macintosh are registered trademarks of Apple Computer, Inc. Sniffy is a trademark of the Governing Council of the University of Toronto. Windows and Excel are registered trademarks of Microsoft Corporation. Reference to these or other products is for informational purposes only, and no endorsement or recommendation is implied.

Library of Congress Control Number: 2004111597

ISBN-13: 978-0-534-63357-8

ISBN-10: 0-534-63357-9

Wadsworth
10 Davis Drive
Belmont, CA 94002-3098
USA

Cengage Learning is a leading provider of customized learning solutions with office locations around the globe, including Singapore, the United Kingdom, Australia, Mexico, Brazil, and Japan. Locate your local office at: **international.cengage.com/region**

Cengage Learning products are represented in Canada by Nelson Education, Ltd.

For your course and learning solutions, visit **academic.cengage.com**

Purchase any of our products at your local college store or at our preferred online store www.ichapters.com

Printed in Canada
5 6 7 8 9 10 11 10 09 08

In memory of Edward Thorndike, Ivan Pavlov, and B. F. Skinner

Contents

Preface: Installing and Running Sniffy Lite ix

Acknowledgments xv

Quick Guide to Menus and Commands xvii

1 Introduction to Sniffy 1

Why We Created Sniffy   1
How We Created Sniffy, the Animated Creature   2
Sniffy, the Program   2
Sniffy Is a Learning Tool, Not a Research Tool   4
Applying What You Learn From Sniffy   5

2 Introduction to Classical Conditioning 7

A First Look at Sniffy Lite   7
Classical Conditioning Background   10
    The Conditioned Emotional Response (CER)   11
The Design Classical Conditioning Experiment Dialog Box   14
The Sensitivity & Fear Mind Window   17
The CS Response Strength Mind Window   18
The Movement Ratio Window   19
The Cumulative Record During Classical Conditioning   20
The Suppression Ratio Window   21
How to Get Reliable, Comparable Results   21
Putting Everything Together to Understand Classical Conditioning   22

Exporting Your Results to Other Programs 23
Printing All the Contents of a Data Window 24
Copying and Pasting the Visible Portion of a Window 24

3   **Basic Phenomena of Classical Conditioning: Acquisition, Extinction, and Spontaneous Recovery** **27**

Important Technical Information 27
Accelerating Time 28
Another Time-Saving Hint 29
Background to the Classical Conditioning Exercises 30
Exercise 1: Basic Acquisition of a CR 30
Exercise 2: Extinction 35
Exercise 3: Spontaneous Recovery 37
Some Questions and Things To Do 39

4   **Introduction to Operant Conditioning** **41**

Edward Thorndike 41
B. F. Skinner 42
The Operant Chamber 45
Reinforcement and Punishment 46

5   **Basic Operant Phenomena: Magazine Training, Shaping, Extinction, Spontaneous Recovery, and Secondary Reinforcement** **51**

Operant Conditioning: Technique 51
The Operant Associations Mind Window 52
Exercise 4: Magazine Training 53
Exercise 5: Shaping Sniffy to Press the Bar 54
If You Have Trouble 58
Exercise 6: Cumulative Records—Visualizing Sniffy's Responding 59
Exercise 7: Extinction 62
Exercise 8: Secondary Reinforcement 67
Exercise 9: Spontaneous Recovery 69
Some Questions and Things to Do 71
Behavioral Repertoire 71
Another Effect of Magazine Training 72

6   **Schedules of Reinforcement and the Partial-Reinforcement Effect** **73**

Background and Examples   73
Variable-Ratio (VR) and Variable-Interval (VI) Schedules   77
Fixed Ratio (FR) Schedules   78
Fixed-Interval (FI) Schedules   78
Setting Up a Schedule in the Design Operant Conditioning
    Experiment Dialog Box   79
Exercise 10: Placing Sniffy on a Small VR Schedule   81
Exercise 11: Increasing the Value of Sniffy's VR Schedule   83
Exercise 12: Variable-Interval Schedules   84
Exercise 13: Fixed-Ratio Schedules   84
Exercise 14: Fixed Interval Schedules   85
How Realistic Are Sniffy's Schedule Performances?   85
Exercise 15: The Effect of Partial Reinforcement on Extinction   86
Some Questions and Things to Do   87
    Does Schedule Size Affect Overall Response Rate?   88
    Does Schedule Size Affect Resistance to Extinction?   88

7   **Shaping Behaviors Other Than Bar Pressing** **89**

Exercise 16: Shaping Sniffy to Beg   91
    If You Have Trouble   92
Exercise 17: Shaping Sniffy to Wipe His Face   93
    If You Have Trouble   94
Exercise 18: Shaping Sniffy to Roll   95
    If You Have Trouble   97
Exercise 19: Shaping Sniffy to Perform Other Behaviors   98
Exercise 20: Shaping a Cat to Beg or Walk on Its Hind Legs   99
Some Questions and Things to Do   101

APPENDIX   **How to Manage Your Sniffy Lite Files** **103**

Floppy Disks and Hard Disks   103
Deciding Where to Save Your Files   105
Getting Easy Access to the Sniffy Program and Files
    From Your Computer Desktop   107
    Creating a Windows Shortcut   107
    Placing Aliases in the Mac OS X Dock   108

Saving Files   109
    Saving Files in Windows XP   109
    Saving Files in Mac OS X   112
Opening Files   113
    Opening Files in Windows XP   113
    Opening Files in Mac OS X   115
Copying Files From a Hard Disk to a Floppy Disk   117
    Instructions for Windows XP Users   117
    Instructions for Mac OS X Users   118
Copying Files From a Floppy Disk to a Hard Disk   119
    Instructions for Windows XP Users   119
    Instructions for Mac OS X Users   119
Using Sniffy Lite Macintosh Files on a Windows PC and Vice Versa   120
Storing Files on a CD   121
E-mailing Files   122

Glossary **124**

References **127**

Index **129**

Preface: Installing and Running Sniffy Lite

System Requirements

Windows

You need an IBM-compatible computer with a Pentium II, or later, processor, running Windows 98 or later, with at least 32 MB of RAM (64 MB recommended), an 8X CD-ROM, a 16 bit sound card with speakers or headphones, and a 600 × 800 color display.

On some computers, the Sniffy Lite program may appear to pause repeatedly while the hard-disk light flashes on and off. This problem occurs when there is not enough RAM available to run the Sniffy Lite program and the computer is attempting to use virtual memory. If this happens, you need to optimize your computer's memory usage by reducing the number of colors displayed. In such cases, we recommend that you set your computer to display 16 bit color. To set your computer's color depth:

- Use your (left) mouse button to open the My Computer window either by selecting on the icon with that name on your Windows desktop or by selecting it from the Start menu.
- Open Control Panel.
- Open Display.
- The details of the appearance of the dialog box vary considerably in different versions of Windows, but somewhere you will find an icon labeled Display. Click on it.
- In the dialog box that opens, look for Settings.
- Choose the setting for 16 Bit Color.

- Click the OK command button in the dialog box.
- Follow any additional instructions that the Windows operating system gives you at this point. It may suggest or require that you restart your computer.

Macintosh

You need an Apple Macintosh computer with a Power PC or later processor, running Mac OS 8.6 or later. The computer must have at least 64 MB of RAM (128 MB recommended), an 8X CD-ROM, an 800 × 600 color display capable of displaying "thousands of colors," a sound card, and speakers or headphones.

Installation

The Sniffy Lite program is designed to be installed on the hard drive of the user's computer. It is not designed to be run from the CD or from a server. Attempting to run the program from the CD or from a server is likely to produce erratic and unpredictable results.

FAQ and Read Me Files

Before installing the program, read the FAQ and Read Me files that are included on your CD. It would also be a very good idea to check the Sniffy Web site to find out whether a revised FAQ file or an update to the Sniffy Lite program is available there. We will post a new FAQ file on the Web site whenever new information becomes available.

Windows

- Use your (left) mouse button to double-click the installer program called Install Sniffy Lite on your Sniffy Lite CD, and follow the instructions as you progress. The first screen that you will see is shown next.

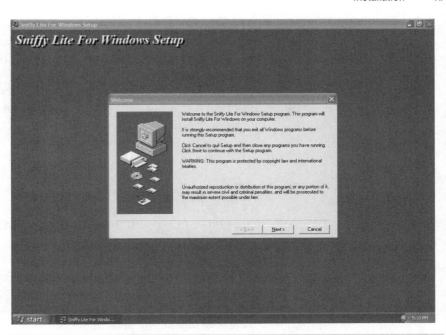

- Click on the Next button.
- In the second screen, you will be asked to enter your name and the name of your organization. For most users, the name of your school would be an appropriate entry for organization.
- In the third screen, you will be asked where on your hard drive you want the installer to place the program. Unless you have a very good reason for selecting another location, accept the installer's suggested destination.
- In the fourth screen, you will be asked whether you want a Typical, Compact, or Custom installation. Almost all users will want a Typical installation.
- The fifth screen asks you to confirm that you want to proceed with the installation.
- Finally, you will see a screen with a progress bar indicating that the installation is in progress. When the installer has completed its work, it will tell you so. You should then exit the installer application.
- The installer will place
  - The Sniffy Lite program and Sample Files folder inside a folder titled Sniffy Lite for Windows that is in the Program Files folder at the root of your C drive.
  - A shortcut to launch the program easily in your Start menu.

■ *You should save all your Sniffy files in your Sniffy Lite for Windows folder so that they are all together in the same place where you can find them easily. When performing the exercises, there will be many occasions when you can save yourself time and effort if you have the file from a previous exercise available to use as the basis for a new exercise.*

Macintosh

All you need to do to install the program on a Macintosh is to copy the Sniffy Lite for Macintosh application from the CD onto your Macintosh's hard drive.

■ If you are running Mac OS X, copy the application from the CD into the Applications folder on your hard drive.
■ If you are running Mac OS 9, copy the application from the CD into the Applications (Mac OS 9) folder on your hard drive.
■ If you are running Mac OS 8, copy the application from the CD into any location on your hard drive except the System Folder.[1]
■ *We also strongly recommend that you create a folder called Sniffy Files on your hard drive and save all your Sniffy files in your Sniffy Files folder. When performing the exercises, there will be many occasions when you can save yourself time and effort if you have the file from a previous exercise available to use as the basis for a new exercise.*
■ If you are running Mac OS X, Apple recommends that you keep all your files in the Documents folder associated with your user name. Thus, the best place for you to create your Sniffy Files folder is inside your own Documents folder. To find your Documents folder:
  □ Double-click on the hard drive icon, which is probably located in the upper right corner of your screen.
  □ Double-click on the Users folder.
  □ Double-click on your own User identity.
  □ Your Documents folder should now be visible.

[1]If you do not know which version of the Mac OS you are running, go to the Apple menu in the upper left corner of your screen and choose About This Mac or About This Computer. The resulting information screen will tell you which version of the operating system you are running.

- If you are running Mac OS 8 or Mac OS 9, you may create your Sniffy Files folder in any convenient location on your hard drive.
- Once you have created your Sniffy Files folder, copy the Sample Files folder from the CD into your Sniffy Files folder. The Sample Files folder contains a number of Sniffy files that you may find useful when you are doing Sniffy exercises.

If you are running Mac OS 8 or Mac OS 9, you must have CarbonLib 1.6 or later installed on your computer. Without it, the Sniffy program will not run. To determine whether you have CarbonLib, go to the Apple menu, control panel, open the Extensions Manager, scroll down to the Extensions section, and look for an entry called CarbonLib. If it's there, the Extensions Manager will tell you what version you have. If you do not have CarbonLib or if the version you have is less than 1.6, the needed file can be downloaded from the support section of the Apple Computer Web site (www.apple.com).

Contacts, Support, and Information

In the United States:

For technical support, visit academic.cengage.com/support or call 800-423-0563.

For order inquiries, call 800-354-9706 or fax your order form to 800-487-8488.

In Canada:

Contact Cengage Learning Nelson—Canada at +1 416.752.9448.

International:

Visit cengage.com/contact/locations/aspx

For the latest information and updates, check out Sniffy on the Web at academic.cengage.com/psychology/sniffy

To contact the authors via e-mail:

Dr. Tom Alloway   antguy@abspruce.org
Dr. Jeff Graham   jgraham@utm.utoronto.ca
Greg Wilson   didsoft@rogers.com

Acknowledgments

We thank the many students, friends, and colleagues who have helped since the inception of this project in 1991. This is the third edition of the software, as we implemented more realistic animations in 2000 and new animations and exercises in 2004. We appreciate the help and support of Professor Doug Chute of Drexel University, who was the first "outsider" to see Sniffy's potential and who helped bring the project to fruition. We thank the CNN, Télée Quebec, and CBC news teams, who helped promote Sniffy as an ethical alternative to the use of live animals in teaching.

Many thanks go to our art director, Allan Sura, for designing and creating the Sniffy movements based on real video of a live rat (although he did have to push the creative envelope for some of the new tricks Sniffy can now perform!). The research assistants in the Psychology Computer Laboratory were our tireless testers. Special thanks go to our testing team, which included Andrew Tomkins, Marie Wong, Nadine Esho, Tiffany Mah, Tracy Lennertz, Luke Kim, Kimberly Chang Alloy, Rafeena Haniff, Edona Caku, Suzana Grozavescu, Vikram Tangri, Roc Scalera, Hubert Marczuk, Mike Hynes, Chris England, Anne Dmitrovic, B. J. Balanquit, Kirk Broadhead, and Keith Seim.

We are grateful to the thousands of introductory psychology students at the University of Toronto at Mississauga who have, over the past 10 years, used early prototypes of the software in class and to the students in Tom Alloway's Introduction to Learning class, who pilot-tested 40 of the exercises used in this edition of Sniffy.

We acknowledge the support of the principal and deans of the University of Toronto at Mississauga, who backed us in the early days before Sniffy attracted the interest of a publisher. We thank the many reviewers who helped refine and polish operational features and pedagogical issues: Jay Allen, University of Georgia; Tim Bockes,

Nazareth College; Victoria Kazmerski, Penn State Erie, The Behrend College; Gail Knapp, Mott Community College; Hal Miller, Brigham Young University; and Nina Tarner, Gettysburg College. Hal Miller's students at BYU did class tests, for which we thank them as well: Jason Allen, Amber Bentzien, Tami Blake, Levi Boren, Matthew Brown, Scott Chamberlain, Danielle Cheesman, Delbert Farley, Jacqueline Gardner, Christopher Gravett, Michael Haderlie, Scott Harrison, Brandon Henscheid, Michelle Hogan, Sarah Johnson, Ben Jones, Elisha Kamalu, Dustin Logan, Kristyn McQuarrie, Amanda Morphy, April Murdock, Jonathan Naylor, Sara Ofahengaue, Amber Orosco, Jessica Pratt, Benjamin Salazar, Jeffrey Skousen, Clinton Snow, Kristen Turley, Michael Turner, and Sonia Yaksich.

Tom Alloway and Jeff Graham congratulate our co-author, Greg Wilson, on his achievement in programming Sniffy for the Macintosh and Windows operating systems. Greg tirelessly tackled the complex assignment of converting psychological principles into demonstrable artificial intelligence and did so while dealing with the complex technical problems of cross-platform development.

Finally, we thank all our Wadsworth editorial team, especially Marianne Taflinger.

Quick Guide to Menus and Commands

This section provides a quick overview of the menu commands in Sniffy Lite. Another description of the principal commands is available in the Sniffy Tutor. The Sniffy Tutor also contains a brief discussion of the program's windows. The Sniffy Tutor illustrates the most common procedures required to save and open Sniffy data files, as well as the menu commands required to set up elementary training and testing scenarios.

The File Menu

New	Ctrl+N
Open	Ctrl+O
Save	Ctrl+S
Save As	
Revert	
Export Data...	
Print Window	Ctrl+P
Preferences...	
Exit	

The File menu contains the standard operating system commands for saving and opening files: **New**, **Open**, **Save**, **Save As**, **Revert**, **Print**, and **Exit (Quit)**. See the appendix to this book if you need detailed information about how to save and open files.

- **New** provides a new rat ready to be trained.
- **Open** brings up the dialog box for opening files.
- **Save** saves the current file under its current name. If the file has not been saved previously, a dialog box appears so that you can give the file an appropriate name and choose an appropriate location on your computer to save it.
- **Save As** brings up a dialog box that enables you to give the file a new name and choose an appropriate location on your computer to save the file.
- **Revert** restores the file to the state it was in the last time you saved it.
- **Export Data** produces a tab-delimited text file containing the data in the currently active window. These data files can be opened in

most spreadsheet and statistical analysis programs. You can use this command with the Cumulative Record, Movement Ratio, Suppression Ratio, DS Response Strength, and CS Response Strength windows.

- **Print Window** prints the currently active window. You can use this command with any window except the Operant Chamber.
- **Preferences** brings up the following dialog box. In Mac OS X, the Preferences command is located under the Sniffy menu.

In the dialog box:

- The **Animate Sniffy** settings control Sniffy's animation when he is visible in his operant chamber.
  - ❑ The settings determine the speed of Sniffy's movements when he is visible in the operant chamber. Clicking a setting toward the left makes Sniffy move more slowly. Clicking a setting toward the right makes Sniffy move faster.
  - ❑ Placing a check mark next to Animate Sniffy causes Sniffy to be visible.
  - ❑ Clicking on the box next to Animate Sniffy to remove the check mark is equivalent to executing the Isolate Sniffy (Accelerate Time) command, which is explained later in the description of commands available under the Experiment menu.
- **Limit Colors To:** enables Macintosh users to control the number of colors displayed in the Sniffy Lite program. The number of colors displayed in other programs is unaffected. This setting is unavailable to Windows users. In Windows, the number of colors displayed is determined by a setting in the Display section of the Control Panel; this setting affects the display of colors in all programs.
- **Sound Proof Cage,** when selected, turns off the program's sound effects. (Selecting this option will make you more popular with your roommates or family!)

The Edit Menu

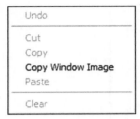

- The **Undo**, **Copy**, **Cut**, **Paste**, and **Clear** commands are not implemented in Sniffy Lite.
- **Copy Window Image** copies a bitmap image of the contents of the currently active window to the clipboard. This command provides a convenient way to insert images from Sniffy Lite windows into a word processor document. To insert an image from a Sniffy Lite window into a word processor document:
  - □ Select the window whose image you want to copy by clicking on the window once with your (left) mouse button.
  - □ Execute the Copy Window Image command.
  - □ Go to the place in your word processor document where you want to insert the image. (If your computer has enough RAM, you can run your word processor and Sniffy Lite at the same time.)
  - □ Select the Paste (or Paste Special) command from the File menu of the word processor program to insert your Sniffy Lite image into the word processor document.

The Experiment Menu

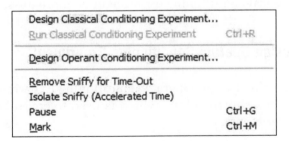

The commands in this menu determine the experimental conditions that are in effect during operant and classical conditioning experiments and control certain other functions.

Design Classical Conditioning Experiment

Executing the Design Classical Conditioning Experiment command brings up the following dialog box. Settings in this dialog box determine the experimental conditions in effect during classical conditioning experiments.

Detailed instructions for using this dialog box are given in Chapter 2.

Run Classical Conditioning Experiment

Executing the Run Classical Conditioning Experiment command causes the Sniffy Lite program to execute a classical conditioning experiment that has been saved in the Design Classical Conditioning Experiment dialog box. The command is dimmed (unavailable) if no classical conditioning experimental design has been specified or if a classical conditioning experiment is in progress.

Design Operant Conditioning Experiment

Selecting Design Operant Conditioning Experiment brings up the dialog box shown below, which is used to control operant conditioning experiments.

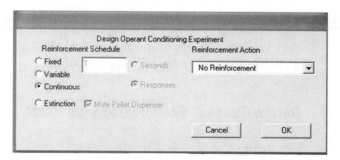

The left side of the dialog box under **Reinforcement Schedule** determines the conditions of reinforcement.

- Selecting **Continuous** causes each response to be reinforced.
- To set up a schedule of reinforcement:
  - Select **Fixed** for fixed-interval (FI) or fixed-ratio (FR) schedules.
  - Select **Variable** for variable-interval (VI) or variable-ratio (VR) schedules.
  - Select **Responses** for ratio (FR or VR) schedules.
  - Select **Seconds** for interval (FI or VI) schedules.
  - The number you type in the text box in this section determines the value of the schedule, in responses for ratio schedules or seconds for interval schedules.
- Selecting **Extinction** causes reinforcement to be turned off. None of Sniffy's responses produce food pellets.
  - Selecting **Mute Pellet Dispenser** eliminates the sound of the pellet dispenser as a consequence of bar pressing.
  - To produce standard extinction conditions, Mute Pellet Dispenser should be selected.
  - If Mute Pellet Dispenser is not selected, Sniffy will continue to hear the sound of the pellet dispenser whenever he responds. Extinction with Mute Pellet Dispenser turned off is used to study the effect of secondary reinforcement.

Remove Sniffy for Time-Out

The Remove Sniffy for Time-Out command brings up the following dialog box.

This command is used in experiments on **spontaneous recovery.** See Chapters 3 and 5 for detailed descriptions of experiments in which the command is employed. In the dialog box:

- Click the OK command button to simulate giving Sniffy a 24-hour rest period in his home cage.
- Click the Cancel command button to dismiss the dialog box without giving Sniffy a rest period.

Isolate Sniffy (Accelerate Time)

The Isolate Sniffy (Accelerate Time) command is available whenever Sniffy is visible. Executing the command replaces the view of Sniffy moving around in his operant chamber with the following graphic:

The graphic depicts the outside of a soundproof, air-conditioned chamber of the type that many psychologists who study operant conditioning use to isolate their easily distracted live animals from extraneous stimuli in the laboratory. Whenever this graphic is visible, your computer will run the current experiment much faster than when Sniffy is visible, because the computer does not have to display Sniffy's movements.

Show Sniffy

The Show Sniffy command is available whenever Sniffy's isolation chamber is being displayed. Executing the command causes the Sniffy animation to reappear.

Pause and Resume

The Pause command is available whenever the program is running. Executing it causes program operation to halt until the Resume command is executed. The Pause command is helpful when something interrupts you while an experiment is running.

Mark (Record)

This command causes a small vertical mark to be placed just below the top of the Cumulative Record window to mark the fact that some event you want to record has occurred. For example, when training Sniffy to bar-press, you might want to mark the record to indicate the time when the Lab Assistant said that Sniffy's training was complete.

The Windows Menu

The commands in the Windows menu make specific Sniffy Lite windows visible. Selecting a window will reopen a window that has been closed or bring to the front any window that is currently obscured by another window. Note that the Cumulative Records and Mind Windows are grouped in separate submenus.

1

Introduction to Sniffy

Why We Created Sniffy

Sniffy Lite is an affordable and humane way to give students hands-on access to the basic phenomena of classical and operant conditioning that introductory psychology courses and courses on the psychology of learning typically discuss. Although psychologists believe that the phenomena that the Sniffy Lite program simulates play a prominent role in both human and animal behavior, courses that discuss these topics are usually taught in a lecture format that gives students no chance to obtain laboratory experience. There are two main reasons for this omission.

The first reason is cost. The most common apparatus that psychologists use to study classical and operant conditioning is the **operant chamber**, a special cage that contains a lever that a rat can be trained to press and devices for dispensing food and water and presenting other stimuli. A computer connected to the chamber automatically records the rat's responses and controls stimulus presentation. A basic setup consisting of an operant chamber, a computer to control it, and an appropriate interface between the two costs about $3,500 in U.S. money. Few schools can afford to purchase this equipment in the quantity required to offer a laboratory component for a course in the psychology of learning. In addition, modern animal-care regulations specify rigorous standards for maintaining animals used for teaching and research. Typically, these regulations not only require that the animals be housed in clean cages and receive adequate food and water, but also specify that animal rooms must receive more fresh air and have better temperature and humidity control than rooms that people occupy. Facilities that comply with these standards are expensive to build and maintain. To cover these costs, animal facilities usually charge daily maintenance fees for each animal kept, and these fees would add up to a large sum if each student enrolled in a learning course had his or her own rat to study.

A second reason why students in learning courses rarely have access to animals is that some people think that the use of live animals for teaching purposes, where the outcome of each experiment can be confidently predicted on the basis of previous findings, violates the ethical principles of humane animal treatment. Some people hold this view even when the animals used for teaching are never exposed to any discomfort. Opposition is much more widespread if the animals are subjected to noxious stimuli.

Nevertheless, studying animal learning without being able to see how experiments are set up and data are collected isolates students from an important and fascinating set of behavioral phenomena. The Sniffy Lite program is designed to end that isolation.

How We Created Sniffy, the Animated Creature

We created the animated Sniffy character that you see on your computer screen by videotaping a live laboratory rat as it moved around spontaneously in a glass cage with a blue background. The taping sessions occurred in a comfortable, reasonably quiet room, and we just let the rat perform whatever behaviors it happened to produce. From the several hours of videotape that we accumulated, we selected 40 short behavior sequences that show the rat walking around the cage, rearing up against the walls, grooming itself, and performing other typical rat behaviors. Finally, we removed the blue background from each frame of these video clips and adjusted the brightness and contrast in the resulting images to produce almost 600 animation frames that depict the rat in different postures and orientations. The Sniffy Lite program plays these frames in various sequences and positions to produce the virtual animal that you see.

Sniffy, the Program

The Sniffy Lite program lets you set up and perform a wide variety of classical and operant conditioning experiments and enables you to collect and display data in ways that simulate how psychologists do these things in their laboratories. In addition, because the program both simulates and displays some of the psychological processes that psychologists believe animals (and people) employ, Sniffy Lite shows you some things about learning that you could not observe if you were working with a live animal.

In a real rat, learning is the result of biochemical interactions among billions of neurons in the brain. As a consequence of these physiological processes, animals acquire information about events in the outside world and about how their behavior affects those events. One aspect of learning involves acquiring information about sequences of events in the world. When one stimulus regularly precedes and thus predicts another, animals modify their behavior in certain ways; psychologists call this kind of learning **classical** (or **respondent**) **conditioning**. A second aspect of learning involves acquiring associations between behaviors (responses) and external events (stimuli); psychologists call this kind of learning **operant** (or **instrumental**) **conditioning**.

Although we believe that neurophysiological processes in the brain are ultimately responsible for the learned changes in behavior that we observe, psychologists generally discuss classical and operant conditioning in terms of the acquisition and modification of associations. To some extent, we describe learning in associative terms because we do not understand the physiological processes well enough to explain our findings fully in physiological terms. However, psychological and physiological processes also constitute different levels of explanation (Keller & Schoenfeld, 1950; Skinner, 1938). Thus, we do not need to understand the physiological processes in detail in order to explain learning in psychological terms.

To a degree, the relationship between neurophysiological processes and psychological explanations of learning is analogous to the relationship between the electrical activity in your computer's electronic circuitry and the simulated psychological processes that form the basis for Sniffy's behavior. Your computer contains the equivalent of several million transistors that are in some ways analogous to neurons in a rat's brain. The Sniffy Lite program uses the electronic circuitry of your computer to simulate the psychological mechanisms that many psychologists employ to explain learning in real animals and people. One advantage of computer simulation is that we can program a computer not only to simulate certain psychological processes, but also to display the simulated processes. This fact has enabled us to develop a set of displays that we call **mind windows**. The mind windows show how Sniffy's behavior interacts with the events in the operant chamber to create, strengthen, or weaken the associations that produce changes in Sniffy's behavior. Thus the Sniffy Lite program not only allows you to set up experiments and record and display behavioral data in a fashion similar to how psychologists do these things, but it also lets you observe how Sniffy's psychological processes operate. We think that being able to observe Sniffy's psychological processes will make it easier to understand how learning works.

Sniffy Is a Learning Tool, Not a Research Tool

The Sniffy Lite program is the result of developments in computer technology that permit the simulation and display of complex processes on relatively inexpensive computers. However, the psychological processes and behavioral phenomena that the program simulates are characteristics of living organisms. Discovering those processes and phenomena required over a century of research with animal and human subjects. Future advances in the scientific understanding of learning will also require research on living organisms. Sniffy Lite and other computer simulations are fascinating tools for demonstrating what we already know, but they cannot substitute for the real thing when it comes to acquiring new scientific insights.

Sniffy is not a real rat. In fact, Sniffy isn't even the most realistic simulation of a real rat that we could have produced. The Sniffy Lite program employs a rat as a kind of metaphor to help you understand the psychology of learning. In designing Sniffy as a learning aid, we deliberately sacrificed realism whenever we thought that it got in the way of creating a useful tool for students. In addition to immediately obvious things like the mind windows, here are some of the other deliberately unrealistic things about Sniffy:

- You will be using food as a reinforcer (reward) to train Sniffy to press the bar or do other things in the operant chamber. Sniffy is always ready to work for food no matter how much he has recently eaten. In contrast, real rats satiate for food and stop working to obtain it when they have had enough. We could have simulated satiation but decided not to because satiation is mainly a motivational, not a learning, phenomenon. If you ever do research using food reinforcement with real animals, you will have to learn how psychologists control for this motivational factor when they design learning experiments. However, textbooks on the psychology of learning rarely discuss satiation, psychological explanations of learning phenomena make little reference to it, and we thought that simulating satiation would introduce a needless inconvenience for students of the psychology of learning.

- Real rats learn some things quite slowly. In an experiment in which an animal is taught to discriminate between the presence and absence of a stimulus by reinforcing bar presses when the stimulus is turned on and not reinforcing bar presses when the stimulus is turned off, a real rat requires many training sessions before the maximum difference in bar-pressing rate in the presence and absence of the stimulus is obtained (Keller & Schoenfold, 1950). In contrast, Sniffy will learn the discrimination in less than an hour. Sniffy also adapts to changes in reinforcement schedules much faster than a real rat. Making Sniffy learn unrealistically fast in these situations gives you time to study more learning phenomena, and we thought that providing the opportunity to study additional phenomena was more important than realistically simulating the speed at which rats learn.

Applying What You Learn From Sniffy

The principles of learning that Sniffy illustrates have many real-world applications in such diverse areas as the therapeutic modification of human behavior and animal training for utility, fun, sport, or profit. In addition to a thorough understanding of learning principles, effectively applying the principles of operant and classical conditioning to real-life situations nearly always involves large measures of creative ingenuity and finesse. To become a practitioner of therapeutic human behavior modification, you need to obtain a bachelor's degree in psychology, attend graduate school, study behavior modification under the direction of a professional, and fulfill the professional licensing requirements of the jurisdiction in which you plan to work. These educational and professional requirements have been established in an effort to ensure the effective and ethical application of the learning principles that Sniffy simulates.

Standards for would-be animal trainers are much less stringent. Anybody can purchase a puppy and attempt to train it. However, if you obtain a puppy and subsequently want to transform the unruly little beast that you actually possess into the obedient, well-behaved member of the household that you had envisioned, you would be well advised to enroll yourself and your puppy in classes at a reputable dog-training school. As with human behavior modification, effective, ethical animal training involves combining a thorough understanding of scientific principles with ingenuity and finesse. The best animal trainers understand both the science and the art. Sniffy will help you learn the science, but you must acquire the art elsewhere. Failure to acquire the art before you try to apply the science can produce unexpected and sometimes even dangerous results.

2

Introduction to Classical Conditioning

A First Look at Sniffy Lite

The time has come to have a look at the Sniffy Lite program and to begin Sniffy's training.[1]

> - Locate the folder where you installed the Sniffy Lite program and sample files on your computer's hard disk.
>   - In Windows, the installer placed Sniffy Lite and the sample files in a folder called Sniffy Lite for Windows, which is in the Program Files folder on your C drive.
>   - On a Macintosh, you should have placed the Sniffy Lite application and sample files in the locations specified in the installation instructions.
> - Start the program.
>   - In Windows, the most basic way to start the program is to select the Sniffy Lite program from the Programs section of the Start menu. Another way is to double-click the Sniffy file icon inside your Sniffy Lite for Windows folder. The Appendix provides information about how to simplify the process of getting to the Sniffy Lite for Windows folder by placing a shortcut to the folder on your Windows desktop.

[1]In this manual, specific, detailed instructions for performing particular exercises are presented with a gray background.

> ▫ On a Macintosh, the simplest way to start the program is to open your Applications folder and double-click the program icon. If you're running Mac OS X, you may want to place an icon for Sniffy Lite and the Sniffy Files folder in the dock. The Appendix provides instructions for placing aliases in the dock.

Depending on whether you're running Sniffy Lite under Windows XP or Mac OS X, when the program opens, your computer screen should resemble one of the following pictures. (If you are running older versions of Windows or the Mac OS, the appearance of the program and its associated windows will be slightly different.)

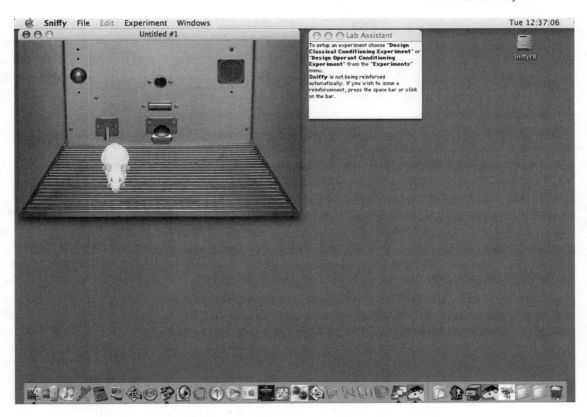

When you first start Sniffy Lite, two windows will be visible:

- The Operant Chamber window is the window where you see Sniffy moving about. The title bar at the top of the window contains the name of the Sniffy file that is currently being run. Because you have not yet saved a Sniffy file, the file is called Untitled.
- The Lab Assistant window provides you with useful suggestions about what to do next or about the status of your current Sniffy experiment. In this instance, it is suggesting that to set up a classical conditioning experiment, you should select Design Classical Conditioning Experiment from the Experiment menu; to set up an operant conditioning experiment, you should select the Design Operant Conditioning Experiment command.

Throughout the rest of this manual, sometimes we will show illustrations of the way the program looks in Windows XP and sometimes show how things look in Mac OS X. Because the program operates identically in both operating systems, always showing illustrations from both operating systems would be redundant.

Classical Conditioning Background

Classical conditioning is the form of learning that results when two stimuli reliably occur in a sequence so that the first stimulus predicts the occurrence of the second. Usually, the stimuli have differing degrees of biological importance to the organism, with the less important stimulus coming before the more important stimulus. Many of the phenomena of classical conditioning were first described by the Russian physiologist Ivan Pavlov and his associates, who were the first to explore this form of learning systematically (Pavlov, 1927). Two other terms for the same kind of learning are **Pavlovian conditioning** and **respondent conditioning**.

In classical conditioning, the stimulus that comes first in the temporal sequence is called the **conditioned stimulus (CS)**, and the stimulus that comes second is called the **unconditioned stimulus (US)**. The US initially possesses the capacity to elicit an obvious, easy-to-measure response called the **unconditioned response (UR)**. The initial response to the CS is called the **orienting response (OR)**, but the OR is often so inconspicuous that psychologists treat the CS as if it were a neutral stimulus that initially elicits no response at all. In other words, the OR to the CS is rarely measured.

The **classical conditioning acquisition procedure** consists of repeatedly presenting the CS shortly before the US. As a consequence of this repeated, sequential pairing of the two stimuli, the CS gradually acquires the capacity to elicit a new learned response, which is called the **conditioned response (CR)**. Usually, but not always, the CR resembles the UR in the sense that the CR consists of certain components of the UR.

In their early experiments, Pavlov and his associates used food placed in the mouths of food-deprived dogs as the US. Food in a hungry dog's mouth elicits chewing, swallowing, and salivation as a UR.

As CSs, Pavlov's group used various medium-intensity sounds, lights, and tactile stimuli, none of which had any initial tendency to elicit a response resembling the UR to food. When repeatedly paired with food presentation, all these CSs gradually acquired the capacity to elicit salivation. During the century since Pavlov first reported his findings, thousands of classical conditioning experiments have been performed, employing dozens of different species and a wide variety of different stimuli as US and CS.

The Conditioned Emotional Response (CER)

Sniffy Lite simulates a form of classical conditioning called the **conditioned emotional response (CER)** or **conditioned suppression**, the experimental paradigm for the measurement of which was first described by Estes and Skinner (1941). Sudden, intense sounds and electric shocks delivered to a rat's feet are stimuli that intrinsically possess the capacity to interrupt a rat's ongoing train of behavior. The rat jumps when the loud sound or shock occurs and then freezes; that is, it remains motionless for a period of time. Thus, very loud noises and foot shock can be used as USs to produce freezing as a UR. In contrast, less intense sounds and moderately bright lights initially have little or no effect on a rat's ongoing behavior. For this reason, these stimuli can be used as CSs. The conditioning procedure consists of turning on the stimulus that is serving as the CS for a period of time before very briefly presenting the US. Usually, the CS and US terminate simultaneously. In different experiments, the period of time during each trial when the CS is presented by itself typically ranges between 30 and 120 seconds (Domjan, 1998, 2003; Mazur, 1998). The duration of the US is usually 1 second or less. As a consequence of pairing the CS with the US, the CS gradually acquires the capacity to interrupt the rat's chain of behavior and induce freezing.

Over the past 30 years or so, the CER has become the form of classical conditioning that North American psychologists most commonly study. There are probably two main reasons for this popularity. First, the CER provides an experimental preparation for studying the acquisition of a very important and interesting response—fear. Second, because the entire process of presenting stimuli and collecting data can be automated, the CER is a very convenient form of classical conditioning to study.

As originally described (Estes and Skinner, 1941) and in most present-day laboratories, studies involving the CER typically start by employing operant conditioning procedures to train a rat to bar-press for food or water reinforcement on a schedule of reinforcement that produces steady, rapid responses (see Chapter 4). The rat's steady bar-pressing rate is then used as a baseline against which to measure the effects of presenting stimuli. However, because almost all textbooks on the psychology of learning discuss classical conditioning before operant conditioning, we thought that it was important to provide users of Sniffy Lite with a means of studying the CER before they learned about operant conditioning. Accordingly, Sniffy Lite enables you to measure fear-related freezing in two ways.

To measure freezing behavior in experiments where Sniffy has not been trained to press the bar, we employ a measurement called the **movement ratio**. This measure is the proportion of time during each presentation of the CS that Sniffy is manifesting freezing and other fear-related behaviors. As the number of times the US has followed occurrences of the CS increases, the proportion of time during the CS when Sniffy will manifest fear behaviors increases. As implemented in Sniffy Lite, the movement ratio provides a robust behavioral measure of classical conditioning *whether or not* Sniffy has previously been trained to press the bar in the operant chamber.

The other way of measuring Sniffy's conditioned fear responses requires that Sniffy first be trained to press the bar in his operant chamber to obtain food reinforcement. This second measure, which is called the **suppression ratio**, is the response measure most commonly used by researchers who study the CER with live rats. The basic idea behind the suppression ratio is to compare the rate of bar pressing (the number of bar presses per minute) during the CS (Rate During CS) to the rate of bar pressing during the period of time immediately preceding presentation of the CS (Rate Pre CS). When the Pre CS and During CS time periods are of equal duration (as in Sniffy Lite), comparing the bar-pressing rates is equivalent to comparing the number of bar presses during the CS (Bar Presses During CS) to the number of bar presses during the period preceding the CS (Bar Presses Pre CS). If the CS elicits no fear response, the number of bar presses during these two time periods should be about the same. However, if the CS suppresses bar pressing, then Bar Presses During CS will be less than Bar Presses Pre CS. To get a quantitative measure of suppression of bar pressing in response to the CS, the suppression ratio is expressed as the ratio between the Bar Presses During CS and the sum of Bar Presses During CS plus Bar Presses Pre CS. Written as an equation, the suppression ratio is defined as:

$$\text{Suppression ratio} = \frac{\text{Bar Presses During CS}}{\text{Bar Presses During CS} + \text{Bar Presses Pre CS}}$$

Let's think a bit about how this equation works. If presenting the CS does not affect the animal's bar pressing (if Bar Presses During CS = Bar Presses Pre CS), then the denominator of the fraction will be twice as large as the numerator; and the suppression ratio will be 0.5. However, if the CS suppresses bar pressing so that the rat presses less during the CS than during the Pre CS period, the suppression ratio will be less than 0.5. If the rat doesn't press the bar at all during the CS, the suppression ratio will be 0. In a CER experiment where the CS is being paired with an aversive US, Bar Presses During CS should never (except by chance) be greater than Bar Presses Pre CS, so that the suppression ratio should generally be less than or equal to 0.5. On the first training trial (before the animal has experienced the US), the suppression ratio should be about 0.5. As conditioning proceeds, the value of the suppression ratio should decline until it eventually levels off at an average value less than 0.5. To compute the suppression ratio, the Sniffy Lite program compares Sniffy's response rate during the 30 seconds preceding each CS presentation with the response rate during the CS.

With real rats and with Sniffy, CER conditioning is rather rapid. Maximal (or nearly maximal) conditioning is reached after about 10 CS–US pairings. The US that the Sniffy Lite program simulates is electric foot shock delivered through the parallel metal bars that form the floor of Sniffy's operant chamber. Shock duration is always 1 second. CS duration is always 30 seconds. When the shock US is being paired with the CS, the shock US occurs during the last second of the CS.[2] Shocking Sniffy immediately interrupts Sniffy's behavior. He jumps and then freezes. When he begins to move around again, bouts of freezing are interspersed with bouts of grooming and exploratory behavior. After a few minutes, the effect of the shock wears off. If Sniffy has been trained to press the bar, bar pressing will resume. If Sniffy has not been trained to press the bar, he will resume moving around the cage and engaging in his other normal activities.

[2]All stated times are in Sniffy Lite program time. Program time is approximately equivalent to clock time when Sniffy's animation is set to run at a realistic-looking rate. However, program time and clock time will seldom be exactly equivalent.

To animate Sniffy's UR to the shock US, we applied some tricks to sequences of animation frames derived from a videotape of a rat that had *not* been shocked or exposed to any other form of noxious stimulation. We think that the result looks plausible, but we do not know how realistic it is. Psychologists who study the CER virtually never give detailed descriptions of their animals' UR to the US. To create a realistic simulation of a rat's response to shock, we would have had to videotape a rat that was actually being shocked, but we did not do that.

The CS that the Sniffy Lite program employs is a light. Duration of the CS is always 30 seconds. On trials when the CS is paired with the US, the US occurs during the last second of the CS. In other words, the onset of the CS always precedes the onset of the US by 29 seconds.[3] The light initially has no effect on Sniffy's bar-pressing performance. However, when a light is paired with the shock US, the light gradually acquires the capacity to suppress bar pressing as a CR. When he is fully conditioned, Sniffy will begin showing bouts of freezing, grooming, and exploratory behavior soon after the light comes on. As was the case with the UR, although we think that Sniffy's CR looks plausible, we do not know how realistic it is because we did not videotape a rat that was actually being conditioned to manifest a CER.

The Design Classical Conditioning Experiment Dialog Box

As noted earlier, one of the reasons for the CER's popularity among North American researchers is the fact that all aspects of CER experiments can be automated. A computer controls the presentation of stimuli, records the rat's behavior, and computes the movement ratio and/or suppression ratio. The Sniffy Lite program provides you with a simplified interface that enables you to set up and run three basic classical conditioning experiments. Like a psychologist in a research lab, you will set up the experiment and then let your computer present the stimuli and record the data. When you choose the Design Classical Conditioning Experiment command from the Experiment menu, the following dialog box appears[4]:

---

[3]All these times refer to Sniffy Lite program time.

[4]The dialog box is shown as it appears in Mac OS X 10.3. In earlier versions of the Mac OS and in Windows, the appearance of the dialog box is slightly different. All the program controls work in the same way in all versions of the Windows and Mac operating systems that the program supports.

Classical Conditioning Experiment Design

┌─View/Edit Experiment Stage 1──────────────────────────────┐

(Next Stage) (Previous Stage)   Interval Between Trials [5] Minutes

(New Stage) (Delete Stage)   Number of Trials   [1]

┌─── First Stimulus ───┐   ┌─── Second Stimulus ───┐

      Light   ⦿ Shock US

                                 ◯ None

(Cancel)   (Save)

Classical conditioning experiments can contain one or more **stages**. A stage is a group of trials. All the trials in one stage are run before any of the trials in the next stage. In the Stage section of the dialog box, the number after View/Edit Experiment Stage indicates which stage of the experiment you are currently viewing. When you first open the dialog box by selecting the Design Classical Conditioning Experiment command from the Experiment menu, the numeral to the right of View/ Edit Experiment Stage will always be 1, indicating that Stage 1 of the experiment is being displayed.

You can edit (create or change) any stage that has not already been run, and you can add more stages to an experiment in which one or more early stages have already been run. You can also view the settings for stages that have been run. However, you cannot change the settings for any stage that has already been run or for a stage that is in the process of being run. When you view the settings for a stage that has already been run or for a stage currently being run, all command buttons are dimmed, and you cannot enter any information into the text boxes.

The Stage section of the dialog box contains four command buttons and two boxes into which you can type numerals:

- If you are viewing or editing Stage 1 of an experiment, the **Previous Stage** command button is dimmed. However, if you are working on Stage 2 or higher, the Previous Stage command is available. Clicking your (left) mouse button when your cursor is on the command button will move you to the previous stage. For example, if you were working on Stage 3, clicking on the Previous Stage button would move you back to Stage 2, and clicking it a second time would move you back to Stage 1.

- The **Next Stage** button moves you from stage to stage in the opposite direction. For example, if you have created three stages and are currently working on Stage 2, clicking the Next Stage button moves you to Stage 3. The Next Stage button is dimmed when you are viewing or working on the last stage that you have defined.
- Clicking on the **New Stage** button creates a new stage, inserts it immediately after the stage that you were viewing when you clicked the button, and automatically moves you to the new stage. If necessary, other stages of the experiment are automatically renumbered. For example, if you have already created three stages and are currently working on Stage 2, clicking on New Stage will create a new Stage 3 and insert it between Stage 2 and the stage that was previously called Stage 3. The former Stage 3 automatically becomes Stage 4.
- The **Delete Stage** button deletes the current stage and, if necessary, automatically renumbers the other stages. Suppose that you have already defined four stages in an experiment and are currently working on Stage 3. Clicking the Delete Stage button will eliminate the old Stage 3 and cause the stage that had previously been called Stage 4 to be renumbered as Stage 3.
- You specify the average time interval between trials for the current stage by typing a number into the **Interval Between Trials** text box. Intervals between trials are measured in minutes. The number you type must be an integer (a whole number without a decimal point). The shortest allowable average interval is 2 minutes; the longest is 20 minutes. Remember that you are specifying the *average* interval between trials. The actual intervals vary from trial to trial so that Sniffy cannot learn to anticipate when the next CS is going to occur.
- The number you type into the box labeled **Number of Trials** determines the number of trials in the stage you are currently editing.

Below the Stage section of the dialog box are sections for defining the first stimulus (CS) and second stimulus (the stimulus, if any, that comes after the CS).

- In Sniffy Lite, the first stimulus is always the light CS, and the duration of the light is always 30 seconds of Sniffy Lite program time.
- There are two possible Second Stimulus settings: Shock US and None.
  - Selecting the Shock US alternative causes the shock to follow each occurrence of the light during the stage you are currently editing.
  - Selecting the None second stimulus alternative causes the light CS to occur without the shock on each trial of the stage you are currently editing.

Two buttons labeled Cancel and Save appear at the bottom of the dialog box.

- Choosing **Cancel** closes the Classical Conditioning Experimental Design dialog box without saving any of the experimental design settings or changes that you have made.
- Choosing **Save** saves the experimental design you have created (or any changes that you have made to the design) as a part of the current Sniffy file.

To run (execute) a classical-conditioning experiment that you have designed, select the **Run Classical Conditioning Experiment** command from the Experiment menu. Once the Run Classical Conditioning Experiment command has been executed, the Sniffy Lite program will run the experiment. *Be sure that the experiment is designed the way you want it before you execute the Run Classical Conditioning Experiment command!*

If you quit (exit) the program or open another Sniffy file after executing the Run Classical Conditioning Experiment command, you will be asked whether you want to save the file. If you save it, the program will begin running the classical conditioning experiment exactly where it left off when you open the file the next time.

If you realize you have made a mistake in setting up a stage of the experiment that has not already started to execute, you can choose the Design Classical Conditioning Experiment command and change the unexecuted stage(s).

The Sensitivity & Fear Mind Window

Below is a picture of the Sensitivity & Fear mind window:

Mind windows display some of the parameters of the Sniffy Lite program that affect Sniffy's behavior. You should view them as representing Sniffy's psychological states. They are *not* measures of Sniffy's behavior. All mind windows have a blue background.

- The column labeled **Pain Sensitivity** depicts Sniffy's sensitivity to the shock US and predicts the strength of his UR the next time the US occurs. This column will always be at its midpoint throughout the experiments in Sniffy Lite.
- The column labeled **Fear** shows the current intensity of Sniffy's fear. Remember that this is not a measure of Sniffy's behavior; it is a measure of an internal psychological process. The more intense Sniffy's internal fear, the more likely he is to display fear behaviors, such as freezing. If Sniffy has been trained to press the bar (or perform any other operantly conditioned response), he will be less likely to display that behavior when he is afraid. If Sniffy has not been trained to perform an operantly conditioned behavior, a high level of fear will reduce his exploratory and other movements that are not related to fear.

The CS Response Strength Mind Window

The CS Response Strength mind window displays the strength of the light CS's capacity to elicit a bar-press suppressing CR as a function of trials. Below is the CS Response Strength mind window as it would be displayed at the end of a one-stage experiment in which the light CS was paired with the shock US 10 times.

Note the following features of this CS Response Strength mind window:

- The blue background color denotes that the CS Response Strength window is a mind window, not a measure of Sniffy's behavior. The psychological state depicted is the strength of the light CS's capacity to elicit a CR at the end of each trial. CS Response Strength predicts how strongly Sniffy will respond to a light the *next* time it is presented.
- The vertical axis of the graph indicates whether the CS Response Strength is excitatory or inhibitory. If a CS has an excitatory, positive tendency to elicit a bar-press-suppressing CR, its response strength will be greater than 0. In Sniffy Lite, the light's CS Response Strength will always be greater than or equal to 0.
- Beneath the horizontal axis of the graph to the right of the word "Stage" is a row of numerals. The numerals denote the stage of the experiment in which each trial occurs. In this example, the row of numerals consists of ten 1's because Stage 1 consisted of 10 trials and was the only stage in the experiment.

The Movement Ratio Window

Below is the Movement Ratio window for this same experiment:

The white background of this window indicates that it contains a measure of Sniffy's behavior. The Movement Ratio is the proportion of time during each CS presentation that Sniffy is frozen or manifesting other fear-related behaviors.

At the bottom of the graph, the row of numbers that appears to the right of the word "Stage" denotes the stage of the experiment.

The movement ratio is 0 on the first trial. After Trial 1, the movement ratio increases rapidly and then levels out at around 0.7.

The Cumulative Record During Classical Conditioning

We believe that most users will be using a file in which Sniffy has not previously been trained to bar-press for their classical conditioning experiments. However, for the benefit of those using files where Sniffy has previously been trained to bar-press, we depict a cumulative record showing how the Sniffy Lite program records events during classical conditioning experiments. Prior to the classical conditioning experiment described earlier, Sniffy had been trained to press the bar in his operant chamber, and his bar-pressing behavior was being maintained on a VR-25 schedule of reinforcement, which means that he had to press the bar an average of 25 times to obtain a pellet of food.

- The characteristics of the cumulative record as a measure of bar pressing and other operantly conditioned behaviors is described in detail in Chapter 5.
- The cumulative record will not contain any useful information unless Sniffy has been trained to bar-press or perform another operant behavior. Users who are not using an operantly conditioned animal for their classical conditioning experiments should ignore this response measure.
- We strongly recommend that users who plan to use an operantly conditioned rat for studies of classical conditioning use an animal that is being maintained on a VR-25 schedule.
- At the left side of the record, near the middle, and on the right side, are the numeral 1 with a short horizontal bar under it, and lettering below the bar that reads "Light: US". The numeral 1 indicates that these three trials occurred in Stage 1 of the experiment. The horizontal bar under the 1 marks the duration of the CS. The lettering below the horizontal bar indicates that the light CS was presented and that it was followed by the shock US.

The Suppression Ratio Window

For the benefit of users who are using an operantly conditioned animal for their classical conditioning experiments, here is the Suppression Ratio window for the same experiment. This response measure produces useful information only for animals that have previously been operantly conditioned.

- The white background of this window indicates that it contains a measure of Sniffy's behavior.
- At the bottom of the graph, the row of numbers that appears to the right of the word "Stage" denotes the stage of the experiment.
- The suppression ratio is about 0.5 on the first trial. After Trial 1, the suppression ratio decreases and then levels out at or just above 0 for the remainder of the experiment. Thus, the light CS acquires the capacity to elicit almost complete suppression of bar pressing.

How to Get Reliable, Comparable Results

The movement ratio is a very robust measure of Sniffy's classically conditioned fear behavior—so robust that it provides a useful response measure whether or not Sniffy has been operantly conditioned to press the bar in the operant chamber or to perform any of the other operantly conditioned behaviors that Sniffy is capable of learning.

However, the suppression ratio depends on measured changes in Sniffy's bar-pressing performance. The Sniffy Lite program computes the suppression ratio by comparing the number of responses that Sniffy makes during the 30-second CS with the number of responses that he makes during the 30-second period just before the CS was presented. To make this measurement reliable, it is critically important that Sniffy be pressing the bar at a rapid, steady rate unless his response rate is being reduced because he is showing either a CR or a UR. If Sniffy is not pressing the bar at a steady rate, you will obtain erratic results because the value of the suppression ratio is affected by the number of bar presses that Sniffy makes during the 30 seconds prior to each CS presentation.

Variable-ratio (VR) schedules produce rapid, steady bar-press performances that make ideal baselines against which to measure suppression ratios. Thus we strongly recommend that you use a VR-trained Sniffy as the starting point for all your classical conditioning experiments that employ the suppression ratio as a response measure. Demonstrating many of the more advanced classical conditioning phenomena that the Sniffy Lite program simulates requires comparing the suppression ratios that Sniffy manifests under different experimental conditions. Whenever such a comparison is necessary, your results will be meaningful only if you use a Sniffy file with the same baseline performance characteristics (a Sniffy trained on the same reinforcement schedule) in each of the different experimental conditions.

The surest way to get predictable, comparable results both within and between experiments using the suppression ratio as a response measure is to use the same baseline Sniffy file as the starting point for all your classical conditioning experiments in which you want to use the suppression ratio as your response measure. The baseline that we used for calibrating the Sniffy Lite program is the VR-25 file located in the Sample Files folder. We recommend that you use it as your classical conditioning baseline in all experiments where the suppression ratio is being used as your classical conditioning response measure. For experiments employing the movement ratio as the response measure, we recommend that you start all your classical conditioning experiment with a new (that is, untrained) Sniffy file.

Putting Everything Together to Understand Classical Conditioning

During a classical conditioning experiment, you can observe four things:

- *Occurrences of the CS and US.*
- *Changes in Sniffy's psychological states.* These changes are visible in the Sensitivity & Fear and CS Response Strength mind windows.
- *Sniffy's responses to the CS and US,* and especially how his response to the CS changes as a function of experience. You can observe

Sniffy's responses to these stimuli simply by watching Sniffy's behavior during and after their presentation.

- *Response measures.* If Sniffy has been trained to bar-press or to perform any of several other automatically recordable operant behaviors, the Cumulative Record contains raw data about occurrences of the chosen operantly conditioned behavior throughout the experiment, shows when the different classical conditioning stimuli occur, and enables you to view the ways in which the stimuli affect Sniffy's operantly conditioned behavior. The Movement Ratio window shows the proportion of time during each conditioned stimulus that Sniffy is manifesting fear behaviors. The Suppression Ratio window contains the classical conditioning response measure that psychologists typically employ in CER experiments.

Being able to see how stimulus events produce psychological changes, which in turn produce behavior changes, which in turn are reflected in behavioral measurements, should enable you to develop a thorough understanding of the way in which psychologists believe classical conditioning works.

Exporting Your Results to Other Programs

During a classical conditioning experiment, the Sniffy Lite program enters data into the Movement Ratio, Suppression Ratio, and CS Response Strength windows. These graphs are saved as part of the Sniffy Lite file so that you can go back and examine your results after an experiment has been completed.

You can also export Suppression Ratio and CS Response Strength results to a spreadsheet or statistical analysis program where you can perform additional data analyses or produce more sophisticated graphs. To export the numeric data on which both the CS Response Strength and Suppression Ratio graphs are based:

- Click your left mouse button once while pointing the cursor at the Movement Ratio, Suppression Ratio, or CS Response Strength window.
- Choose the Export Data command from the File menu. Executing the Export Data command will bring up the standard dialog box for creating and saving a new file.

- Choose an appropriate name and location on your hard drive for your data export file and click OK.

Printing All the Contents of a Data Window

You can print the contents of any response measure or mind window that the Sniffy Lite program produces.[5] To print the contents of a window:

- Select the window by placing the cursor over it and clicking your left mouse button once.
- Execute the Print Window command in the File menu.
- Make the necessary selections in the printing dialog box that appears.

Copying and Pasting the Visible Portion of a Window

With the exception of the Operant Chamber and the Lab Assistant, the visible portion of all the windows that the Sniffy Lite program produces can be copied and then pasted into a word-processing or graphics program that accepts pasted images. To copy and paste the visible portion of a Sniffy window:

- Open your word-processing or graphics program and determine where you want to paste the image that you are going to copy from Sniffy Lite. In a word processor, it's a good idea to go to the place in your document where you want to insert the image and to create a blank line there.
- Open the Sniffy Lite data file containing the window whose image you want to copy.
- If necessary, make the window that you want to copy visible by selecting it from the Windows menu.
- Make sure that the window that you want to copy is selected by clicking on it once.

[5] The only window whose contents *cannot* be printed is the operant chamber, the window in which you see Sniffy moving around.

- Execute the Copy Window command in the Sniffy Lite program's Edit menu.
- Move back to your word processor or graphics program.
- Execute the word processor's or graphics program's Paste command, which will probably be under that program's Edit menu. (Some programs have a special paste command for pasting images.)
- The graphic contents from the Sniffy Lite window will appear in the other program's document.

3

Basic Phenomena of Classical Conditioning: Acquisition, Extinction, and Spontaneous Recovery

Important Technical Information

❖ In the following exercises, the instructions for saving Sniffy Lite files direct you to select an appropriate destination *on your computer's hard disk*. It is extremely important that you get into the habit of saving your Sniffy Lite files on the hard disk of the computer that you are using. *Never save a file on a floppy disk.* Sniffy files can grow to be quite large. If you try to save a large Sniffy file on a floppy disk that does not have enough room to accommodate it, the program will not be able to save the file successfully. As a consequence, the time and effort that you have invested in doing an exercise may be lost. This potential problem results from the limited storage capacity of floppy disks. It is *not* a problem with the Sniffy Lite program. Similar problems arise with any program that produces large files.

❖ If your instructor wants you to hand in your Sniffy Lite files on floppy disks, you should initially save the files on your computer's hard disk and then copy the saved files from the hard disk onto one or more floppy disks.

❖ If you do not have your own computer and must therefore store your Sniffy Lite files on floppy disks, you should initially save the file on the hard disk of the computer that you're using, then copy the files onto one or more floppy disks. You should then copy the files from the floppy disks back onto the hard disk of the computer that you're using before you try to work with the files again.

❖ You need to keep track of where you save your Sniffy Lite files on your computer's hard disk so that you can find them easily when you need to. A very good place to keep them is in the Sniffy Files folder that was installed on your hard drive when you installed the program.

❖ If you require additional information about saving files, see the Appendix at the back of this manual.

Accelerating Time

Some of the Sniffy Lite experiments that you will be performing require an hour or two of both clock time and program time to complete when your computer is displaying all Sniffy's movements. To enable you to run long experiments faster, we have made it possible for you to make Sniffy invisible so that your computer can run the experiments as fast as possible. Selecting the **Isolate Sniffy (Accelerate Time)** command from the Experiment menu simulates enclosing Sniffy's operant chamber in a sound-proof, air-conditioned container of the type used in many laboratories to isolate an easily distractible live animal from extraneous stimuli that might divert the animal's attention from the experiment itself. When he is hidden, the window in which Sniffy is normally visible will look like this.

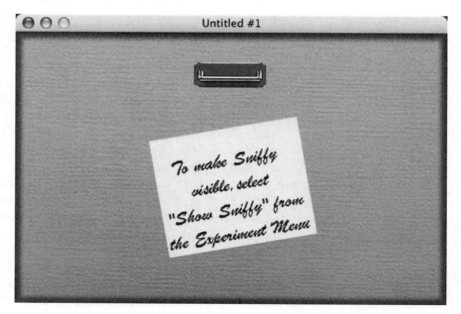

The amount of time acceleration that isolating Sniffy will achieve depends on the speed of your computer. With a relatively slow computer,

5 minutes of program time may pass in 90 seconds. With a fast computer, 5 minutes of program time may be compressed into 5 seconds or less. To make Sniffy visible again, click on the handle in the isolation window or choose the **Show Sniffy** command from the Experiment menu. The Isolate Sniffy (Accelerate Time) and Show Sniffy commands replace each other in the Experiment menu: The Isolate Sniffy (Accelerate Time) command is available whenever Sniffy is visible; the Show Sniffy command is available whenever Sniffy is isolated.

Warning: Don't let accelerated time get away from you. *If you are running an experiment using time acceleration and want to be able to add new stages to the experiment later, you need to keep an eye on things and stop the experiment when the exercise you are currently performing is complete. There is a time limit of 20 hours of program time for each Sniffy experiment, at which point no more data can be collected. If your computer can run an experiment 20 times faster than clock time when Sniffy is isolated, an hour of program time will elapse in 3 minutes. Unless you watch what's going on, it's easy to run an experiment for several "hours" longer than you intended.*

The Sniffy Lite program includes two useful features to help you avoid running a time-accelerated experiment longer than you intended:

- The program signals the end of a classical conditioning experiment by beeping at the end of the last currently programmed classical conditioning trial. When you hear that sound, save the file and either quit (exit) the program or set up the next exercise that you want to perform.
- The Lab Assistant informs you about the status of your experiment. When a classical conditioning experiment is in progress, the Lab Assistant window provides several kinds of self-explanatory information about what is going on. When the classical conditioning experiment is complete, the Lab Assistant's message will change.

Another Time-Saving Hint

If your computer has enough random access memory (RAM), you can set up a Sniffy exercise and let the program run the experiment in the background while you do something else on your computer. The program will run more slowly in the background than in the foreground, but that speed difference may be offset by the convenience of being able to do something else while the program is performing an experiment.

Background to the Classical Conditioning Exercises

Acquisition (learning) of a classically conditioned response is produced by repeatedly presenting the CS followed by the US. As a result of this acquisition procedure, the CS gradually acquires the capacity to elicit a new response (CR) that in most forms of classical conditioning resembles the UR. Once a classically conditioned response has been acquired, it can be eliminated by repeatedly presenting the CS alone, without the US. Elimination of CR by repeatedly presenting the CS without the US is called **extinction**. If the animal is removed from the experimental situation for a day or so after a CR has been extinguished and then returned to the experimental setting and given a second extinction session, it is likely that CR will occur again during the first few trials of the second extinction session. This reappearance of a previously extinguished CR is called **spontaneous recovery**. Early in the second extinction session, the CR is stronger than it was at the end of the first extinction session but weaker than it was at the end of acquisition.

Exercise 1: Basic Acquisition of a CR

Acquisition is produced by setting up a series of trials in which a CS regularly precedes occurrences of the US. The following steps describe how to set up and run an experiment in which Sniffy receives 10 pairings of the light CS with the shock US.

- If you plan to use the movement ratio as your measure of classical conditioning, simply start the Sniffy Lite program or, if the program is already running, choose the New command from the File menu.
- If you want to employ the suppression ratio as a response measure, open a file in which Sniffy has been fully trained to bar press on a VR schedule. We recommend that you copy the file

named VR-25 that is located in the Sample Files folder, and use it as the baseline file for this and all your classical conditioning experiments that employ the suppression ratio as a response measure.

- □ Use the Save As command in the File menu to save the file under an appropriate new name (for example, Ex1-ClassAcq) on your computer's hard drive. We strongly recommend you save it in the Sniffy Files folder that the installation instructions directed you to create in an appropriate place on your hard drive. If you are running the Macintosh version of the program, the Sniffy Files folder that we asked you to create on your hard drive when you installed the program is the best place to keep all your Sniffy files. If you are running the Windows version of the program, we suggest that you save this exercise and all future exercises in the Sniffy Lite for Windows folder that the installer program created. That folder is inside the Program Files folder at the root level of your hard drive.[1]

- Choose the Design Classical Conditioning Experiment command from the Experiment menu. In the Classical Conditioning Experiment Design dialog box, do the following:
  - □ Note that the numeral 1 appears after View/Edit Experiment Stage. This indicates that you are setting conditions for the first stage of the experiment.
  - □ Make sure the numeral 5 appears in the text box located to the right of Interval Between Trials, indicating that the average interval between trials will be 5 minutes.
  - □ In the text box located to the right of Number of Trials, type 10.
  - □ In the Second Stimulus panel of the dialog box, make sure that the shock US is selected.
  - □ Carefully check to see that all the settings are correct.
  - □ Click the Save command button.

- After the Experimental Design dialog box has closed, choose the Run Classical Conditioning Experiment command from the Experiment menu.

- If you want to speed up execution of the experiment, select the Isolate Sniffy (Accelerate Time) command from the Experiment

---

[1]If you need additional information about how to save files, see the Appendix at the back of this manual.

menu. If you use this feature, be careful not to let the program run very long after the experiment is completed. You will need the file that this exercise creates in the next exercise.

■ After the last acquisition trial, save your results by selecting the Save command from the File menu.

During the next 50 minutes of program time, the program will automatically run the experiment. While the program is running, the Movement Ratio window will draw a bar graph that shows Sniffy's movement ratio as a function of trials. At the same time, the CS Response Strength mind window will produce a line graph depicting changes in the CS's capacity to elicit a CR.

At the end of the experiment, your Movement Ratio and CS Response Strength windows should resemble the following:[2]

[2]The CS Response Strength mind window shown here is from Windows XP. If you are running another version of Windows or the Mac OS, the contents of the mind window should look exactly like that shown, except for the format of the window borders. The contents of mind windows depict processes that are parts of Sniffy's learning algorithm, and these parameters are completely determined by the settings that you make in the Classical Conditioning Experiment Design dialog box. However, the resemblance between the Movement Ratio window shown and the one you get will be less exact. The movement ratio is a measure of Sniffy's actual behavior. As Sniffy learns, the learning algorithm changes the *probability* that Sniffy will behave in certain ways, but does not completely determine what Sniffy does. Because the learning algorithm only changes the probabilities with which behaviors occur, the details of the movement ratio result will be different each time the experiment is performed.

During acquisition, the movement ratio starts at 0 on the first trial, then rises and levels off at about 0.7. This increase in the movement ratio means that the light CS is acquiring the capacity to induce freezing and other fear-related behaviors. At the same time the movement ratio is increasing, the CS Response Strength mind window shows that the light's capacity to elicit fear as a psychological process is also increasing. Remember that the Movement Ratio window depicts a change in Sniffy's behavior, while the CS Response Strength mind window depicts the change in Sniffy's psychological state that influences the behavioral change.

If you performed the experiment with a file in which Sniffy had previously been trained to bar-press, the Suppression Ratio window should resemble that shown here:

During acquisition, the suppression ratio starts out at around 0.5 on the first trial, then declines and levels off at an average value a little above 0. This decrease in the suppression ratio means that the light CS is acquiring the capacity to suppress Sniffy's bar pressing. You could verify this fact by examining the cumulative record. During the last several trials, you would note that Sniffy stops pressing the bar very quickly after the light comes on.

With a real rat, the animal's changing response to the CS would be the only thing that a psychologist could observe. Many psychologists explain this behavior change by postulating that it results from a change in an unobservable psychological process. With the conditioned emotional response, the acquired capacity of a CS to elicit freezing and to suppress bar pressing or other operantly conditioned behaviors is thought to be the result of an increasingly intense fear response. During CS presentations, Sniffy's Sensitivity & Fear mind window displays the strength of Sniffy's current fear, and the CS Response Strength mind window shows how strong the fear response will be when the CS is presented the next time. With Sniffy Lite, you can observe both the behavior change and the change in the Sniffy Lite program's classical conditioning algorithm, Sniffy's psychological state, that causes Sniffy's behavior to change. We have designed Sniffy's classical conditioning algorithm to resemble theoretical processes that psychologists (for example, Guthrie, 1960; Hull, 1943, 1952; Rescorla & Wagner, 1972) have postulated in an effort to explain classical conditioning. However, nobody has ever seen anything closely analogous to CS Response Strength in a rat's brain, and many psychologists assert that it's impossible, even in principle, to observe the psychological (mental) processes of real animals. We believe that the Sniffy Lite program's mind windows will help you understand psychological explanations of classical conditioning, but it's important to remember that they do not provide any deep insights into the workings of the "animal mind."

An interesting point to note is that the movement ratio and suppression ratio measures of Sniffy's response to the CS are not a perfect reflection of Sniffy's internal fear response. As the CS Response Strength and the Sensitivity & Fear mind windows show, Sniffy's fear response is at an almost constant high level during the last several acquisition trials. Yet the value of Sniffy's movement ratios and suppression ratios fluctuate somewhat from trial to trial. These behavioral measures vary because Sniffy's behavior is determined by a complex set of probabilities. Changes in Sniffy's learning algorithm (Sniffy's psychological state) change the *probabilities* with which fear-related behaviors occur, but Sniffy's behavior is always probabilistic and somewhat variable.

These variations in Sniffy's movement ratio and suppression ratio are somewhat analogous to the results that you obtain if you repeatedly perform an experiment in which you toss a coin 10 times. On any given coin toss, the probability that the coin will come up heads is equal to the probability that it will come up tails. For this reason, if you perform a great many 10-toss experiments, the average number of heads will be 5; however, the exact number of heads will vary from experiment to experiment. Sometimes you will get 5 heads, sometimes 7 heads, and sometimes 4 heads. The operation of similar processes accounts for the variation that you see in Sniffy's response measures. The response measures vary because Sniffy's behavior is probabilistic. After every movement Sniffy makes, there are several things that he could do next. His experiences in the operant chamber change the probabilities of his behaviors, but the program is designed in a way that ensures that we can never know in advance exactly what Sniffy will do next. Even under very similar conditions, Sniffy doesn't always do the same thing. This variability in Sniffy's behavior is what accounts for the variability that we see in the classical conditioning response measures. The behavioral measures that psychologists obtain with real animals vary in a similar fashion and possibly do so for somewhat similar reasons.

Exercise 2: Extinction

These instructions assume that you have already run the acquisition experiment described in Exercise 1. To set up a series of 30 extinction trials, you should follow the steps listed below. You need to conduct more extinction trials than acquisition trials because the CER extinguishes much more slowly than it is acquired.

- Start the Sniffy Lite program and open the file that we suggested you name Ex1-ClassAcq, in which Sniffy acquired a CR to the light CS.
- Use the Save As command to save the file under a new name (e.g., Ex2-ClassExt) in the Sniffy Files folder on your computer's hard drive.
- Choose the Design Classical Conditioning Experiment command from the Experiment menu. The Classical Conditioning Experiment Design dialog box opens to Stage 1. All the options for defining conditions are dimmed because Stage 1 has already been run.
- In the Classical Conditioning Experiment Design dialog box, make the following settings to define Stage 2, which will contain your extinction trials:
  □ Click on the command button labeled New Stage. The number after View/Edit Experimental Stage changes from 1 to 2 to indicate that you are now working on Stage 2 of the experiment. Because this is a new stage that has not yet been run, all the options are available.
  □ In the Stage section, be sure that the numeral 5 appears in the text box after Interval Between Trials, and type 30 in the text box located to the right of Number of Trials. These settings indicate, respectively, that the average interval between trials will be 5 minutes and that there will be 30 trials.
  □ In the Second Stimulus panel, choose None.
  □ Carefully check your settings.

□ Click on the Save button at the bottom of the dialog box to save the experimental design.
- After the Classical Conditioning Experiment Design dialog box closes, choose the Run Classical Conditioning Experiment command from the Experiment menu.
- If you want to speed up the experiment, select the Isolate Sniffy (Accelerate Time) command from the Experiment menu. Because you will need to use the file from this exercise as the starting point for the next exercise, you want to avoid inadvertently letting the program run for very long after this exercise is complete.
- When the program has finished running the experiment, choose the Save command from the File menu to save your results.

During the next 150 minutes of program time (less if you choose Isolate Sniffy), the Sniffy Lite program will automatically give Sniffy 30 extinction trials—that is, 30 trials during which the CS occurs without the US. As the program executes, the Sniffy Lite program will draw a graph showing Sniffy's movement ratio on each trial in the Movement Ratio window and the strength of the light's capacity to elicit fear at the end of each trial in the CS Response Strength window. At the end of extinction, your Movement Ratio and CS Response Strength windows should resemble the following:

The Movement Ratio window shows that repeatedly presenting the CS without the US causes the CS to gradually stop eliciting freezing and other fear-related behaviors. The CS Response Strength mind window shows that this behavior change is the result of the CS's losing its capacity to elicit a fear response. Once again note the variability in the movement ratio that reflects the probabilistic nature of Sniffy's behavior. If your experiment was performed on a file in which Sniffy had been trained to bar-press, the Suppression Ratio window should look something like the following:

Exercise 3: Spontaneous Recovery

Here are the steps that you need to follow to observe spontaneous recovery:

- Open the file that we suggested you call Ex2-ClassExt from Exercise 2, in which Sniffy was first conditioned in Stage 1 and then extinguished in Stage 2.
- Use the Save As command to save the file under an appropriate new name (e.g., Ex3-ClassSponRec) in the Sniffy Files folder on your computer's hard drive.
- Under the Experiment menu, choose Remove Sniffy for Time Out. This operation simulates removing Sniffy from the operant chamber, leaving him in his home cage for 24 hours, and then returning him to the experimental situation.
- Choose Design Classical Conditioning Experiment from the Experiment menu and make the following settings in the Classical Conditioning Experiment Design dialog box to give Sniffy a second 15-trial extinction session:
  - The dialog box opens (as always) to Stage 1. All alternatives for defining trials and stimuli are dimmed because Stage 1 has already been run.
  - To define a new Stage 3, you must first move to Stage 2 because new stages are always inserted immediately after the

stage currently being displayed. Click on Next Stage to move to Stage 2, which has also already been run.

- □ When you reach Stage 2, click on New Stage to create the new Stage 3 after Stage 2. Note that the numeral 3 is now present after View/Edit Experiment Stage.
- □ Ensure that the Interval Between Trials is set at 5 minutes.
- □ Set Number of Trials to 15.
- □ In the Second Stimulus panel, choose None.
- □ Carefully check your settings.
- □ Click on the Save command button at the bottom of the dialog box to save the experimental design.
- ■ After the dialog box closes, choose the Run Classical Conditioning Experiment command from the Experiment menu.
- ■ If you want to speed up the experiment, select the Isolate Sniffy (Accelerate Time) command from the Experiment menu.
- ■ When the experiment has finished running, save the file.

As Stage 3 executes, the movement ratio will be graphed as a function of trials in the Movement Ratio window, and the strength of the light's capacity to elicit a fear response will be graphed in the CS Response Strength mind window. At the end of the experiment, these two windows should resemble those shown next:

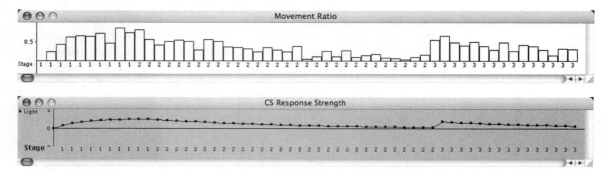

If your Sniffy was trained to bar-press on a VR schedule, your Suppression Ratio window should resemble the following:

Some Questions and Things To Do

- Compare and contrast the movement ratio and the suppression ratio as response measures in classical conditioning.
- As the strength of an animal's fear response increases, the value of the movement ratio increases, but the value of the suppression ratio decreases. Why? How can two measures of the same thing move in opposite directions as the strength of the thing measured increases?
- Why do you think that most psychologists studying live rats use the suppression ratio and not the movement ratio as their response measure?

4

Introduction to Operant Conditioning

Edward Thorndike

The research that led to the study of what today we call operant conditioning began over a century ago with the work of Edward Thorndike. Impressed by William James's classic textbook, *Principles of Psychology* (James, 1890), Thorndike enrolled at Harvard University and took courses with James. At Harvard, Thorndike began the first experimental study of learning in animals. At the time, there was no formal psychological laboratory at Harvard and very little money to support Thorndike's work. His first laboratory was in his home.

Thorndike (1898) described his early animal learning experiments in a classic monograph. In these experiments, Thorndike studied the way cats learned to escape from an apparatus that he called a **puzzle box**. The cats were locked inside the box and had to manipulate a mechanical device to open the box and escape. Initially, the cats behaved in many different ways, most of which did not lead to escape. However, gradually by trial and error, the cats found the behaviors that led to escape. Thorndike recorded how long it took each cat to escape on each trial and found that the average time gradually decreased from several minutes to a few seconds. As the escape speeds increased, the cats were learning to eliminate useless behaviors, while retaining the much smaller number of successful behaviors. The form of learning that Thorndike studied is often called **instrumental conditioning**. Thorndike summarized the mechanism that strengthens and selects successful behaviors by stating what he called the **law of effect**:

> Of several responses made to the same situation, those which are accompanied or closely followed by satisfaction to the animal will, other things be-

ing equal, be more firmly connected with the situation, so that, when it recurs, they will be more likely to recur; those which are accompanied or closely followed by discomfort to the animal will, other things being equal, have their connections with that situation weakened, so that, when it recurs, they will be less likely to occur. The greater the satisfaction or discomfort, the greater the strengthening or weakening of the bond. (quoted in Kimble, 1961, p. 10)

Thorndike's experiments showed that the effect—the consequence—of a behavior determines whether the behavior will be strengthened or weakened. Hitting the right combination of levers in Thorndike's puzzle box had the positive effect of opening the door and letting the cat out of the box. As with most pioneers, Thorndike's models of instrumental conditioning and his statement of the law of effect have been subject to many changes. However, they remain an important cornerstone of our understanding of the learning process.

B. F. Skinner

B. F. Skinner formulated methods and procedures that describe a variant of Thorndike's instrumental conditioning that Skinner called **operant conditioning**. In Thorndike's work with puzzle boxes and subsequently in his studies of animals learning to run mazes, the learning tasks involved apparatus and procedures in which animals had the opportunity to make a correct response only at certain well-defined times called **trials**. Skinner developed a learning situation in which an animal is confined during training in a cage called an **operant chamber**, which contains a device on which responses can be made as well as a mechanism, called the **magazine**, for the delivery of food. In an operant chamber, animals are trained in an experimental situation in which the opportunity to perform some response is continuously available. Like Thorndike, Skinner was interested in how the consequences of behaviors influence the frequency with which those behaviors are repeated. Skinner's work with operant conditioning is thus an extension of Thorndike's work with instrumental conditioning. Moreover, the same principles of learning seem to apply both when the animal has the opportunity to make a correct response only at certain times (as in Thorndike's puzzle boxes and mazes) and when the animal is able to respond at any time (as in Skinner's operant chamber).

Skinner (1938) made three fundamental assumptions about behavior:

- Animals are frequently active, a fact that means that organisms are continually **emitting** various behaviors.
- These emitted behaviors frequently have consequences that influence the frequency with which the behaviors are repeated in the future.
- The effects of the consequences are influenced by the animal's motivational state as well as by the physical and social environment. For example, the effect of presenting food as a consequence of performing some behavior depends upon whether the animal has been deprived of food.

Skinner studied animal learning, but he believed that it was possible to apply his findings to design more effective human institutions in which the planned, systematic application of reinforcement would make people happier and more productive (Skinner, 1953). Skinner not only called for the objective study of behavior, but also posited that behavior is often caused by events in the environment that can be discovered and manipulated to change behavior; in other words, he attempted to create a philosophical framework based on his findings. This effort generated a lot of excitement and controversy (Skinner, 1971).

Traditionally, people have believed that mental events cause many aspects of human behavior. In contrast, Skinner (1953, 1971) asserted that it is more useful to view feelings, thoughts, emotions, and most other mental events as covert behaviors. In Skinner's view, both overt behaviors and the mental events that accompany them occur because of current and past conditions of reinforcement; and both are subject to the same behavioral laws.

Although he recognized that behavior is produced by the interaction of genetic and environmental factors, Skinner and his followers have concerned themselves almost exclusively with environmental effects. The historical reasons for this emphasis on the environment are complex; but one important reason is that environmental factors are easier to manipulate than genetic factors, especially in human beings, in which genetic manipulations are usually considered to be unethical. For example, a child's genes and the environment in which the child grows up jointly determine how tall the child will grow to be. However, although nothing can be done about a child's tallness genes once the embryo has been conceived, the diet that the child eats—an environmental factor—can significantly affect adult height.

Skinner (1938, 1953) stated that psychologists should be concerned with discovering the laws of behavior and emphasized the importance of relating environmental causes to behavioral effects. In addition, he believed it is often possible to discover behavioral laws without understanding what goes on inside the organism. Many psychologists have employed the metaphor of a black box to characterize this aspect of Skinner's approach to psychology. The box, which represents the organism, is opaque. The inside is invisible, and we don't need to know what goes on inside the box. Understanding the rules that govern the box's behavior and controlling its actions do not require opening it. In fact, trying to understand what goes on inside the box may be confusing and misleading.

We can understand this black box view of the individual by considering the behavior of a television set. Few of us can produce or understand a circuit diagram that explains how a TV set works, but we can still operate one. We know that we must plug the set into an electric outlet. We know that when we manipulate the channel selector, the stations change. We know that a second control adjusts the volume, and other controls change the colors. The picture and sound are the behaviors that we want to predict and change, and we can predict and change these behaviors. If the set is not working properly, we also know that sometimes a sharp rap on the side of the case will improve the picture. None of this knowledge about how to change the behavior of a TV set requires understanding its internal workings. Skinner believed we can predict and change the behavior of organisms, including ourselves, in a similar way without needing to understand the internal workings of the body.

Skinner (1938) proposed that psychologists should seek to discover relationships between the environment and behavior without speculating about what goes on inside the organism. However, this "agnostic" approach to the workings of the organism was one of the most controversial aspects of Skinner's approach to psychology. A great many psychologists in Skinner's day (such as Guthrie, 1960; Hull, 1943, 1952; Tolman, 1932) believed, and a majority of present-day psychologists still maintain, that understanding behavior requires understanding the psychological and/or physiological processes that go on inside the organism. A computer program manual is not the place to debate these profound issues in the philosophy of science. Suffice it to say that in designing a virtual animal that simulates the behavior of a real rat in an operant chamber, we had to endow Sniffy with certain psychological processes in order to reproduce the results that Skinner and others have obtained. Sniffy's psychological processes are modeled after those discussed in many contemporary textbooks on the psychology of learning (for example, Domjan, 1998; Mazur, 1998; Tarpy, 1997). Nevertheless, there is no way of knowing how closely Sniffy's psychological processes resemble those of real rats. All we can say is that Sniffy's psychological processes, which we display in the various mind windows, illustrate the kinds of processes that many psychologists believe are characteristics of real rats.

Skinner (1935, 1938, 1953) distinguished between elicited and emitted behaviors. An elicited behavior is the specific result of presenting a particular stimulus. You studied how learning can affect elicited behaviors in the preceding experiments on classical conditioning. In contrast, emitted behaviors are responses that occur without any readily identifiable eliciting stimulus. For example, there is no stimulus that will reliably elicit grooming movements or barking from all normal dogs in the same way that placing food on a dog's tongue will elicit salivation.

Many of the behaviors that psychologists are interested in understanding are emitted, not elicited. Consider the behavior of students during class. Students not only listen to the instructor and take notes, but also scratch, yawn, doodle, wiggle around in their seats, and exhibit a wealth of other behaviors. Almost all these behaviors are emitted in the sense that no single stimulus exists whose presentation will reliably elicit any of these behaviors from everyone.

The scientific question to which Skinner sought experimental answers was, What controls the frequency of emitted behaviors? To address this question, Skinner developed the operant chamber, a very simple environment in which he thought it would be possible to discover how the environment determines the frequency with which animals and people produce emitted behaviors.

The Operant Chamber

Sniffy's operant chamber resembles those found in laboratories where psychologists do research on operant conditioning. A look at Sniffy's operant chamber reveals three particularly important objects on the back wall: a lever, or so-called **bar**, that you will train Sniffy to press; a water spout; and a food hopper. As in all operant conditioning situations, the bar is continuously available for Sniffy to press. The hopper is the device that you will use to provide a positive consequence, or **reinforcement**, when Sniffy does something that you want him to do more often. You can program the operant chamber to deliver food pellets automatically when Sniffy presses the bar, or you can dispense pellets manually by hitting the space bar on your computer keyboard or by clicking your computer's (left) mouse button while pointing at the bar. Other devices in Sniffy's operant chamber permit you to present other kinds of stimuli. These include a speaker through which sounds might be played, a light that can be turned on and off, and the parallel metal bars that form the floor through which electric shocks can be delivered.

In this restricted environment, a real rat performs a limited subset of species-typical behaviors. As with a real rat, you can expect to see Sniffy rearing up, grooming himself, and exploring the chamber. You can observe and record many of Sniffy's behaviors. However, the response that psychologists generally study in an operant chamber is bar pressing. In research laboratories, psychologists use computers to control the presentation of food and other stimuli and to record bar presses, and the Sniffy Lite program simulates these functions.

Reinforcement and Punishment

Skinner (1938) defined **reinforcement** as a procedure that makes a behavior pattern, or **response**, more likely to be repeated under similar circumstances in the future. In operant conditioning, the term *rein-*

forcement refers to the procedure of presenting or removing a stimulus (called a **reinforcer**) as a consequence of performing a response. A **positive reinforcer** is a stimulus whose presentation as a consequence of a behavior causes that behavior to occur more frequently under similar circumstances in the future. The term **positive reinforcement** refers to the procedure of presenting a positive reinforcer as a consequence of a behavior pattern. You will use food as a positive reinforcer to train Sniffy to press the bar or do certain other things in the operant chamber. A **negative reinforcer** is a stimulus whose removal or termination as a consequence of a behavior makes that behavior more likely to occur under similar circumstances in the future. The term **negative reinforcement** refers to the procedure of removing a negative reinforcer as a consequence of a behavior. Uncomfortable environmental conditions (temperature extremes, rain) are examples of negative reinforcers—stimuli whose termination can strengthen behaviors. As the saying goes, most people are smart enough to learn to come in out of the rain. Both positive and negative reinforcement have the effect of increasing the rate (the number of times per minute or hour) at which the reinforced response will occur under similar circumstances in the future.

Skinner (1953, 1971) decried the fact that much of our society is controlled by negative reinforcement. If we have a noisy neighbor in an apartment building, we may bang on the wall to make the noise stop. Termination of the annoyance is negative reinforcement for wall banging and will increase the probability of banging the wall again under similar circumstances in the future. Children do homework to avoid parental nagging, a woman visits her mother to escape her husband's abusive behavior, a worker shows up for work on time to avoid unemployment. Skinner believed that this heavy reliance on negative reinforcement is a sign of a poorly planned society. He wrote several books and articles describing how society might be better organized based on knowledge of operant principles and extensive use of positive reinforcement.

Operant conditioning also defines two procedures for punishing behavior. **Punishment** is the mirror image of reinforcement. Whereas reinforcement causes behaviors to be repeated more often, punishment causes behaviors to occur less often. A **positive punisher** is a stimulus whose presentation following the occurrence of a response makes that response occur less often in the future. **Positive punishment** is the name of the procedure involved in presenting a positive punisher as a behavioral consequence. If you hit your puppy with a rolled-up newspaper when it has a toilet accident in the house, you are employing positive punishment. A **negative punisher** is a stimulus whose removal following a response causes that response to occur less often in the future. **Negative punishment** is the procedure involved in removing a negative punisher to make a behavior occur less often. If your daughter misbehaves while watching her favorite television program and you send her to her room (thereby terminating access to the television program), you are employing negative punishment.

Note that the terms *negative* and *positive* have the same meaning when applied to punishment that they have when applied to reinforcement. Both positive reinforcers and positive punishers have their effects respectively of strengthening or weakening behaviors when you *apply* or *turn on* the stimuli following a behavior pattern. Thus, the term *positive* in this context refers to the presentation or application of a stimulus. Both negative reinforcers and negative punishers have their respective effects when the stimuli are *removed* or *terminated*. Thus, the term *negative* in this context refers to the removal of a stimulus. But remember: Both positive and negative reinforcement cause behaviors to occur more often, whereas both positive and negative punishment cause behaviors to occur less often.

Another dimension that applies to both reinforcers and punishers concerns whether the reinforcing or punishing power of the stimulus is intrinsic or learned. Food is a good example of a stimulus whose reinforcing power is intrinsic in the sense that animals require no special training in order for food to acquire the capacity to act as a positive reinforcer. Similarly, presenting electric shock is an intrinsic positive punisher, and terminating shock is an intrinsic negative reinforcer. Stimuli whose effectiveness as reinforcers or punishers requires no special training are said to be **primary reinforcers** or **primary punishers**. Other stimuli that lack intrinsic reinforcing or punishing power can acquire the capacity to act as reinforcers or punishers if they are paired with primary reinforcers or punishers. Money is a good example of a stimulus whose reinforcing power has been acquired in this way. There is nothing intrinsically reinforcing about money; it's just pieces of paper and metal disks. However, people learn to treat money as a powerful positive reinforcer because of its pairing with primary reinforcers such as food and drink. Stimuli that acquire reinforcing or punishing power as a result of pairing with primary reinforcers or punishers are called **secondary**, or **conditioned**, **reinforcers** or **punishers**.

In operant conditioning, organisms learn that particular behaviors produce particular consequences in particular situations. In more technical terms, many psychologists believe that operant conditioning involves learning a three-part association among a situation, a response, and a reinforcing or punishing consequence (Domjan, 1998; Mazur, 1998; Schwartz & Reisberg, 1991; Tarpy, 1997). The effect of reinforcement is to select for the reinforced behavior at the expense of other unreinforced behaviors. In other words, the effect of reinforcement is to make the reinforced behavior occur more often; a side effect of reinforcement is that many unreinforced behaviors occur less often because the animal or person comes to perform the reinforced behavior so frequently that less time is available to do other things. The effect of punishment is just the opposite of that of reinforcement. Punishment selects against the punished behavior, thereby making it occur less often and, as a side effect, making other unpunished behaviors occur somewhat more often. An animal's **behavioral repertoire** is a list of all the behaviors that the animal would ever produce. The effect of operant conditioning is always to modify the relative frequencies with which different behaviors in the behavioral repertoire occur.

Skinner argued that punishment, in either of its forms, is undesirable for several reasons. Apart from ethical considerations, perhaps the most important of these reasons is that punishment is a less effective training tool than reinforcement because punishment conveys less information. When you punish an animal or child for doing something, you are in effect teaching the subject not to perform one particular item in its behavioral repertoire in the situation where the punishment occurred, but punishment provides no information about which other behaviors are appropriate. Reinforcement is a more powerful training tool because reinforcement specifically teaches the organism what to do.

5 Basic Operant Phenomena: Magazine Training, Shaping, Extinction, Spontaneous Recovery, and Secondary Reinforcement

Operant Conditioning: Technique

Like a real rat, Sniffy will occasionally press the bar in the operant chamber even before you train him to do so. Thus, when you condition Sniffy to press the bar, you are not teaching him to do something that he was previously incapable of doing. Reinforcement simply increases the frequency with which bar pressing occurs. To train Sniffy to bar-press, you will administer a food pellet for each bar press. Thus, you will be using positive reinforcement to train Sniffy.

From what we've said so far, you might think that all you need to do to train Sniffy to bar-press is to set up the operant chamber so that the magazine releases a food pellet each time Sniffy presses the bar. In fact, if that's all you do, Sniffy will eventually learn to press the bar; but he will take rather a long time to do so. The reason for this slowness illustrates one of the most basic principles of operant conditioning: To be effective, reinforcement must occur *immediately* after the response. Delayed reinforcement is much less effective. The problem with food as a reinforcer in this situation is that even though a food pellet drops into the food hopper as soon as Sniffy presses the bar, the food can have no effect on Sniffy until he finds it; and Sniffy may not find the food immediately. When he does find it, the food will strengthen whatever behavior Sniffy was performing just before he found it, and that is much more likely to be sniffing around the hopper than bar pressing.

Food is a very effective reinforcer that can be used to train animals to do many kinds of things, but it is often hard to deliver food fast enough to reinforce effectively the response that the trainer wants to strengthen. To overcome this difficulty, animal trainers often transform a stimulus whose timing they can precisely control into a secondary reinforcer by associating that stimulus with food. Then the trainer uses the secondary reinforcer to increase the frequency of the response that the trainer wants the animal to learn. Fortunately, the magazine in an operant chamber produces a distinctive mechanical sound when it drops a food pellet into the hopper; it is easy to transform this sound, which has no intrinsic power to act as a reinforcer, into a secondary reinforcer by pairing the sound with food delivery in a way that causes Sniffy to associate the sound with food presentation. The procedure that turns the magazine sound into a secondary reinforcer is called **magazine training**.

The Operant Associations Mind Window

The Operant Associations mind window displays the strength of three associations that Sniffy will learn when you train him to press the bar. To display the Operant Associations mind window, click on the Windows menu and then select Operant Associations from the Mind Windows submenu. In an untrained Sniffy, the Operant Associations mind window looks like this:

The **sound–food association** is the association between the sound of the food pellet-dispensing mechanism and the fact that a pellet of food is available in the hopper. You will teach Sniffy this association during the next exercise on magazine training. The **bar–sound association** is the association between the bar and the sound produced by the food-dispensing mechanism. When Sniffy is trained to press the bar, Sniffy learns that the bar is the device whose manipulation causes the sound that signals the presence of a food pellet in the hopper. **Action strength** is Sniffy's association between a particular behavior pattern and obtaining food. A strong sound–food association is a prerequisite for training Sniffy to perform any operant behavior. Action strength will also develop whenever Sniffy is trained to perform any operantly conditioned behavior.[1] However, the bar–sound association develops only when Sniffy is trained to bar-press. The bar–sound association doesn't develop when Sniffy is trained to do something other than bar pressing because none of the other behaviors that Sniffy can be operantly conditioned to perform involves doing anything with the bar.

Exercise 4: Magazine Training

Magazine training is a technique that involves using what amounts to a classical conditioning procedure to turn an originally neutral stimulus into a *secondary reinforcer*.[2] The training process involves an interaction between you and Sniffy. What you will do depends on what Sniffy does, and Sniffy's future responses to the magazine sound will depend on what you do. The idea is to operate the magazine to present pellets of food in such a way that Sniffy learns to associate the sound of the magazine with the availability of a food pellet in the hopper. One of the associations that the Operant Associations mind window displays is the sound–food association. By keeping an eye on the Operant Associations mind window, you can watch Sniffy develop an association between the magazine sound and food.

Here are the steps that you need to follow to magazine-train Sniffy:

- Start with a new Sniffy file.
- Use the Save As command in the File menu to save the file under an appropriate name (e.g., Ex4 MagTrain) in the Sniffy Files folder.
- Display the Operant Associations mind window by selecting it from the Mind Windows section of the Windows menu.
- The message in the Lab Assistant window reads, "To set up an experiment, choose Design Classical Conditioning Experiment or Design Operant Conditioning Experiment from the Experiment menu. Sniffy is not being reinforced automatically. If you with to issue a reinforcement, press the space bar or click on the bar." The last sentence of the Lab Assistant message is the relevant instruction for this experiment.

[1]In Chapter 7, we will show you how to train Sniffy to perform several other behaviors.
[2]Chapter 4 defines and discusses the concept of secondary reinforcement.

- Wait until Sniffy closely approaches the food hopper. Then deliver a food pellet either by pressing the space bar on your computer keyboard or by pointing the cursor at the bar and clicking your (left) mouse button.
- To save time at the start, you may want to give Sniffy several pellets in rapid succession before he wanders away from the hopper.
- After Sniffy has received several pellets, you can let him wander away a short distance before giving him the next pellet.
- Keep an eye on the Operant Associations mind window. When the height of the sound–food bar reaches about one quarter of the way up the scale, the message in the Lab Assistant window will change to read, "Sniffy is developing an association between the sound of the hopper and the presentation of food. However, this association is not strong enough to properly train Sniffy. Continue to present food when Sniffy is near the hopper." Follow the Lab Assistant's advice. Continue to reinforce Sniffy when he is near the hopper.
- Because you will want to be able to use this file as the basis for training Sniffy to perform several different behaviors, during magazine training do not consistently give Sniffy a food pellet after he performs any particular behavior or category of behavior.
- When the height of the sound–food bar in the Operant Associations mind window reaches about three quarters of the way up the scale, the Lab Assistant will display the message, "Sniffy appears to have developed an association between the sound of the hopper and the food. You can now use the sound as a reinforcer to shape Sniffy's behavior."
- Sniffy's magazine training is now complete.
- Save the file.

Exercise 5: Shaping Sniffy to Press the Bar

After magazine training, if the operant chamber is programmed to drop a pellet of food into the hopper every time Sniffy presses the bar, Sniffy's occasional spontaneous bar presses will be effectively reinforced, and Sniffy will learn to bar-press all by himself if you just leave him alone. Moreover, he will do so much more quickly than would have been the case without magazine training. However, if you are observant and have a good sense of timing, you can accelerate this learning process by using a technique called **shaping**.

Shaping is the technical name of the procedure employed to train an animal to do something by reinforcing successive approximations of the desired **target behavior**. Shaping is a procedure in which the trainer (teacher) leads the subject (learner) to progress by small steps. Reinforcement is delivered for progress and then withheld until more progress has been made.

To be a successful shaper, you have to be a careful and patient observer. Shaping works because behavior is variable. The idea is to pick a behavior that the animal performs fairly often and that is similar in some way to the target behavior you want the animal to perform eventually. Reinforcing this first approximation of the behavior will cause Sniffy to perform that behavior more frequently. Because Sniffy's behavior is composed of movements that occur with different probabilities, you will notice a number of different variations. Eventually, Sniffy will perform a variant of the behavior that more closely resembles the target behavior. That variant then becomes your second approximation, and you require him to repeat that variant to obtain reinforcement. As the second approximation is performed more frequently, Sniffy will eventually emit another variant that resembles the target even more closely, and so on.

Shaping an animal takes patience, careful observation, and good timing. It is a skill that you learn with practice. Sniffy is easier to shape than a real rat partly because he never becomes satiated for food and partly because his behavioral repertoire is smaller than a real rat's. Nevertheless, shaping Sniffy is challenging enough for you to get some idea of both the frustration and the eventual feeling of triumph that shaping an animal engenders.

In the Sniffy Lite program, bar pressing is part of a **response class** (a group of similar movements) in which Sniffy lifts his front paws off the floor while facing the back wall of the chamber. We programmed Sniffy that way because, in order to press the bar, Sniffy must first go to the bar and then rear up in front of it. Thus, as your first approximation to bar pressing, try reinforcing Sniffy for rearing up anytime he is facing the back wall of the chamber on which the bar and food hopper are mounted. Once rearing up facing the back wall has become more frequent, require him to rear up with his feet against the back wall. If your patience, observational skills, and timing are good, you should have Sniffy bar pressing frequently in less than 30 minutes. If you are very skillful, you can shape Sniffy in less than 15 minutes. However, if you are inattentive or have bad timing, you might have been better off letting Sniffy learn to bar-press on his own after magazine training.[3]

Shaping is such an attention-demanding task that you should not pay attention to anything but Sniffy's behavior while you are shaping. However, once Sniffy has pressed the bar four or five times in a minute, you can stop shaping him and watch the progressive effect of reinforcement as Sniffy presses the bar more and more often. At that point, you should start keeping an eye on the Operant Associations mind window in order to observe the development of bar–sound association and action strength. The bar–sound association tells Sniffy that the bar is the device he uses to produce the sound that signals the delivery of a food pellet. The action strength is the degree to which Sniffy has learned that pressing is what he does with the bar to get the sound that signals the delivery of a food pellet.

Here is a detailed description of the steps that you should follow to shape Sniffy to press the bar:

- Open the file from Exercise 4 that we suggested you call "Ex4 MagTrain."
- Select the Save As command from the File menu to give the file an appropriate new name (such as Ex5 ShapeBP) and save it in the Sniffy Files folder on your computer's hard drive. *Saving the file with a new name before you start shaping Sniffy preserves your original magazine-training file for future use.* You will need it for a number of subsequent exercises.
- If the Operant Associations mind window is not already visible, display it by selecting it from the Mind Windows section of the Windows menu.
- If Cumulative Record 1 is not visible, make it visible by selecting it from the Cumulative Record section of the Windows menu.
- Select the Design Operant Conditioning Experiment command from the Experiment menu.
- In the dialog box that appears, select Bar Press from the Target Behavior section of the drop-down menu under Reinforcement Action. After making the selection, click on OK to close the dialog box.

[3]Psychologists who study operant conditioning in live rats approach shaping in a variety of ways. Some people start the shaping process by reinforcing the rat whenever it approaches the bar. Others begin by reinforcing the rat whenever it turns toward the bar. Some of these alternative approaches also work well with Sniffy.

- Note that the terms CRF and Bar Pressing appear in the cumulative record. CRF stands for Continuous Reinforcement, which means that the program will automatically reinforce every bar press. The Bar Press notation indicates that the cumulative record is recording bar presses.

- As your first approximation to bar pressing, give Sniffy a pellet of food when he rears up facing the back wall anywhere in the operant chamber.

- Gradually require Sniffy to rear up closer and closer to the wall.

- Whenever Sniffy rears up directly in front of the bar, there is a chance that he may press it. If he does press the bar, he will hear the magazine sound, receive a food pellet, and the bar–sound association will start to develop. After several reinforced bar presses, a red column will appear above the words Bar-Sound and Action Strength in the Operant Associations mind window.

- When the column above Bar-Sound in the Operant Associations mind window reaches about one quarter of the maximum height, the message in the Lab Assistant window will change to read, "Sniffy is developing an association between the bar and the sound. Continue and Sniffy should be trained soon."

- Each time Sniffy presses the bar, watch closely what he does after eating the food pellet. He may press the bar again a second time either immediately or after rearing up near the bar a time or two. If he does press the bar again, you know you're making progress. Allow him to continue pressing the bar as long as he will do so. However, if he rears up more than twice without pressing the bar again, continue to reinforce rearing up.

- If you are patient, the time will come when Sniffy will press the bar 8 to 10 times in rapid succession. At that point, you can stop shaping, sit back, and watch the progressive effect of reinforcement as Sniffy continues to press the bar more and more frequently.

- Watch the rising levels of the Bar-Sound and Action Strength columns in the Operant Associations mind window. Sniffy's training is complete when the message displayed by the Lab Assistant changes to read, "Sniffy appears to be trained properly. You may experiment with different schedule effects."

- When Sniffy is fully trained, select the Save command from the File menu to preserve your trained Sniffy for future use.

If You Have Trouble

After 30 to 45 minutes of attempting to shape Sniffy according to the instructions just given, Sniffy should be pressing the bar *at least* 20 times during each 5-minute interval delineated by the alternating solid and dotted vertical lines in the cumulative record.

If your attempt at shaping fails to obtain that minimum result, something is wrong. One possibility is that Sniffy has not been properly magazine trained. Look at the Operant Associations mind window. The Sound-Food association level should be *more than* three quarters of the way up the scale. If it isn't, either go back and repeat Exercise 4 to create a properly magazine trained Sniffy or use the file entitled MagTrain from the Sample Files folder.

A second possibility is that you may not be reinforcing instances of rearing up toward the back wall as outlined earlier or not reinforcing these behaviors quickly enough.

If you are having trouble reinforcing Sniffy's rearing behaviors, we have provided a section of the Reinforcement Action menu in the Design Operant Conditioning dialog box called the **Shaping Tutor** to help you.

- Choose the Design Operant Conditioning Experiment command from the Experiment menu.
- Under the Shaping Tutor subsection of the Reinforcement Action menu, choose Rear Up Facing Back.
- The Sniffy Lite program will now automatically reinforce all instances of rearing up facing the back wall, including all bar presses. Watch which actions the program automatically reinforces.
- When you believe that you are capable of effectively reinforcing these behaviors manually, reopen the Design Operant Conditioning Experiment dialog box and choose Bar Press from the Target Behaviors section of the Reinforcement Action menu.
- If you are unable to reinforce Sniffy effectively by hand, watch what is going on as the program reinforces rearing up facing the back wall automatically. Once Sniffy presses the bar 8 to 10 times in a 1- or 2-minute period, reopen the Design Operant Conditioning Experiment dialog box and choose Bar Press from the Target Behaviors section of the Reinforcement Action menu. The program will complete Sniffy's training automatically.

- When the Lab Assistant displays the statement "Sniffy appears to be trained properly. You may experiment with different schedule effects," save the file.

Exercise 6: Cumulative Records—Visualizing Sniffy's Responding

In this exercise, you will learn how to interpret **cumulative records**, the means of recording and displaying a rat's bar-pressing behavior that B. F. Skinner (1930) invented. Although there is nothing specific for you to do with Sniffy in this exercise, we suggest you read the following paragraphs while seated in front of your computer with the program running so that you can look at Sniffy's cumulative record from time to time to check out the various features that we are going to describe.

- If the Sniffy Lite program is not running, start it.
- Use the Open command from the File menu to open the file that we suggested you name Ex5 ShapeBP in Exercise 5.
- If the latest cumulative record isn't visible, display it by selecting it from the Cumulative Responses submenu of the Windows menu.
- Note that as time passes, the visible part of the cumulative record automatically scrolls to the right to follow Sniffy's current behavior. If you want to look at something that happened earlier, you can use the scroll bar at the bottom of the window to scroll back to the left.

How do we know whether a rat has learned anything as a result of training in the operant chamber? With Sniffy, you can observe the learning process directly in the Operant Associations mind window. However, when dealing with real animals whose psychological processes are invisible, psychologists treat learning as a process whose operation they must infer solely on the basis of changes in behavior.

Because bar pressing becomes more frequent as a result of training, Skinner chose to measure learning in the operant chamber as an increase in the frequency of bar pressing. To make the necessary measurements, he invented the **cumulative recorder**. Skinner's cumulative recorder was a mechanical device that pulled a long roll of paper at a constant speed under a pen that rested on the moving paper. At the start, the pen was positioned at the bottom of the record; if the rat did not press the bar, the pen would simply draw a long, straight horizontal line. However, every time the rat pressed the bar, the pen moved a notch upward toward the top of the paper. When the rat was pressing the bar, the resulting record was a sloping line that moved from the bottom edge toward the top of the record. The more rapidly the rat responded, the steeper the slope of line. In other words, Skinner's cumulative recorder drew a record in which the steepness of the line was directly proportional to the rate of bar pressing.

The roll of paper that Skinner used in his cumulative recorder was not very wide. After recording a certain number of responses, the slanted line would reach the top edge of the paper. When that happened, the pen very quickly reset to the bottom edge of the paper, causing a vertical line to be drawn across the paper from top to bottom. This pattern of a slanted line working its way to the top of the paper, followed by a sharp straight line to the bottom of the page, gives a cumulative record the appearance of mountain peaks or waves.

These days, mechanical cumulative recorders of the sort that Skinner invented are obsolete. Scientists who study operant conditioning use computers to draw cumulative records of bar pressing in a fashion similar to the way the Sniffy Lite program produces them. We have described the workings of Skinner's original mechanical device because we think its operation is easier to understand than that of a computer program that simulates the device.

There are several important things to remember about the cumulative records that the Sniffy Lite program produces and about cumulative records in general:

- The slope of the rising lines on the graph represents the speed with which Sniffy is responding. The steeper the slope, the more rapidly Sniffy was pressing when the record was made. If Sniffy is pressing the bar slowly, the slanted line will take a long time to reach the top of the paper where it resets to the bottom. This will result in a record that looks like gentle, undulating waves. If Sniffy is pressing fast, the slanted line will reach the top faster, the pen will have to reset more often, and the resulting record will look like more and steeper "waves."
- Reinforced responses are marked by short, oblique lines drawn through the record.
- If you let it run long enough, the Sniffy Lite program will produce a series of 10 Cumulative Record windows. The Cumulative Record

windows, which are called Cumulative Record 1, Cumulative Record 2, and so on, are accessible under the Cumulative Records section of the Windows menu.

- Each Cumulative Record window depicts Sniffy's bar-pressing performance during 2 hours of Sniffy Lite program time. *Program time and clock time are not the same thing.* The relationship between program time and clock time depends on both the speed of your computer and the animation speed setting. You can adjust the animation speed in the dialog box that appears when you execute the Preferences command under the File menu.[4] When the animation speed has been adjusted so that Sniffy is moving at a rate that looks realistic, program time and clock time should pass at approximately the same rates.

- The fact that there is a maximum of 10 Cumulative Record windows means that no Sniffy experiment can last more than about 20 hours in program time. After that program time limit has been reached, you can examine and save your results, but you cannot add any stages to that particular Sniffy Lite file.

The cumulative record depicted here shows the acquisition of bar pressing as a consequence of shaping in a "typical" experiment. No two cumulative records are ever exactly alike, because Sniffy never behaves in exactly the same way in any two experiments. However, if you were a successful shaper, the part of your cumulative record from Exercise 5 that recorded Sniffy's acquisition of the bar-pressing response should resemble the one shown. Here are some characteristic things about the record shown above that you can expect to see in your own cumulative record:

- The flat, horizontal portions of the line show periods when Sniffy was not pressing the bar.

[4] The Preferences command is under the Sniffy menu in Mac OS X.

- Sniffy begins to press the bar slowly and intermittently at first, then more and more frequently and steadily.
- Note that the steepness of the cumulative record increases rather rapidly at first and then more slowly. A similar increase in the rate of bar pressing should be visible in your record. However, its relationship to pen resets is likely to be different.
- In addition to depicting Sniffy's response rate and showing which responses were reinforced, the cumulative records that the Sniffy Lite program produces denote the times at which a variety of other significant events occur during experiments. We will explain these additional features in connection with descriptions of experiments where they are important.

Here are a couple of important features that are specific to the cumulative records that the Sniffy Lite program produces:

- The "height" of Sniffy's cumulative record is always 75 responses. There are always 75 responses between any two consecutive pen resets. When the pen resets the first time, Sniffy has made 75 responses. When it resets the second time, he has made 150 responses, and so on. Knowing this will come in handy later on when you need to figure out how many responses Sniffy has made.
- In addition to the dark vertical lines that the cumulative record produces when the pen resets from the top of the record to the bottom, there are thinner, alternating solid and dotted vertical lines spaced at regular intervals. These thinner vertical lines are 5-minute time markers. The time between one thin vertical line and the next (between a solid line and the next dotted line or a dotted line and the next solid line) is 5 minutes in Sniffy Lite program time; the time between two successive solid or two successive dotted vertical lines is 10 minutes in program time.

Exercise 7: Extinction

After training Sniffy to press the bar, you might wonder what would happen if you stopped reinforcing bar presses. This sounds like a simple question, but it reflects some of the complexity of life in a world where food sources come and go. Animals need to be flexible. They need to be able to learn what to do to obtain whatever food happens to be available at the moment, and they need to be able to stop doing things that no longer produce food. **Extinction** is the technical name for the behavior changes that occur when a previously reinforced behavior no longer produces reinforcement.

Here is what you need to do to set up and run an extinction experiment:

- If the Sniffy Lite program is not running, start it.
- Use the Open command under the File menu to open the file containing your trained Sniffy from Exercise 5.
- Use the Save As command to save the file under an appropriate new name (such as Ex7 Ext for extinction) in the Sniffy Files folder on your computer's hard drive. *This step is quite important because it preserves your original trained Sniffy file for future use.* You will need your trained Sniffy file for other exercises.
- Choose the Design Operant Conditioning Experiment command from the Experiment menu. Executing this command opens the following dialog box:

- When the dialog box opens, the button labeled "Continuous" and the reinforcement action "Bar Pressing" are selected because you have been reinforcing all of Sniffy's bar-press responses. Reinforcing every response is a procedure called **continuous reinforcement**.
- To select extinction, point the cursor at the radio button labeled "Extinction" and click your left mouse button.
- Be sure there is a check mark in the box next to Mute Pellet Dispenser. (If the check mark isn't there, place the cursor over the

box and click your (left) mouse button to put a check mark in the box.) Setting up extinction with Mute Pellet Dispenser selected means that Sniffy's bar presses will no longer produce food pellets and that he will no longer hear the magazine sound as a consequence of bar pressing. In other words, both the primary reinforcer (food) and the secondary reinforcer (the magazine sound) are turned off. This is the standard extinction procedure.

- After checking to be sure that you have made the correct settings, click the OK command button.
- After you click OK, the dialog box will disappear, and the Sniffy Lite program will begin running again, but Sniffy's bar presses will no longer be reinforced. Immediately after you click OK, your cumulative record will look something like the one shown here:

- If you want to speed up the experiment, select the Isolate Sniffy (Accelerate Time) command from the Experiment menu.
- Note that the Sniffy Lite program marks the cumulative record to show the point at which extinction starts and informs you that the magazine sound is muted.

As a consequence of stopping reinforcement, Sniffy's rate of bar pressing will eventually decline until he presses the bar no more often than he did before he was trained. However, the first effect of extinction is to increase Sniffy's bar-pressing rate. This increase in response rate is called an **extinction burst**, and it commonly occurs when an animal is switched from continuous reinforcement to extinction.

Your extinction criterion is a 5-minute period during which Sniffy presses the bar no more than twice. When that point is reached, you should:

- Mark the cumulative record by executing the Mark Record command in the Experiment menu.
- Save your extinction file by selecting the Save command from the File menu.

When the extinction criterion is reached, you should estimate the number of responses that Sniffy made between the onset of extinction and the time when the criterion was reached. You should also estimate the time required to reach the extinction criterion.

When estimating the number of responses and the time elapsed during extinction, remember that:

- The thin alternating dotted and solid vertical lines on the cumulative record mark off 5-minute periods in program time.
- Sniffy always makes 75 responses between two successive pen resets.

Determining how many responses Sniffy has made during extinction and the time that extinction required will typically call for you to estimate fractional parts of 75-response vertical pen excursions and fractional parts of 5-minute time intervals. You can elect either to make precise measurements or to do "eyeball" estimates.

If you want to make precise measurements, you should print your cumulative record and make the appropriate measurements with a ruler. To print your cumulative record:

- Select the Cumulative Record window by pointing the cursor at it and clicking your left mouse button once.
- Select the Print Window command from the File menu.

To do an "eyeball" estimate, look at the cumulative record and estimate the appropriate horizontal (time) and vertical (response) movements as a proportion of 5-minute intervals and 75-response vertical pen excursions.

For example, have another look at the cumulative record shown on page 64, which displays the point at which the change from continuous reinforcement to extinction occurred.

The change occurred partway through a 5-minute interval between two vertical lines and partway up from the bottom of the cumulative record.

- With regard to time, the change occurred not very long before a vertical line marking the end of a 5-minute interval. Let's say that it occurred about 4/5 or 80% of the way through the 5-minute interval. Four-fifths of 5 is 4, so our estimate is that the change occurred about 4 minutes into the 5-minute interval, so that about 1 minute remained before the cumulative record reached the time marker.

- With regard to the number of responses that Sniffy made after the previous time marker and before the switch to extinction, it looks as though the cumulative record had moved no more than two or three responses up from the bottom. We know that there are 75 responses between pen resets, so this means that he had about 72 or 73 responses to go before the pen reset again.

A couple of aspects of the standard extinction experiment are worthy of some discussion. One of them is the *extinction burst*, the increase in response rate that occurs immediately after Sniffy (or a real rat) is switched from continuous reinforcement to extinction. With real animals, the concept of *frustration* is sometimes evoked as an explanation. An animal that has become accustomed to continuous reinforcement expects to be reinforced for every response. When the expected reinforcement fails to occur, frustration, a hypothetical emotional state, results. This emotion supposedly energizes the animal to make a burst of responses.

With Sniffy, the explanation is much simpler. Sniffy does not manifest frustration. We know this because we did not model frustration in the Sniffy Lite program. When Sniffy is being maintained on continuous reinforcement, he hears the magazine sound after each bar press and comes down off the bar to eat the pellet of food whose availability the magazine sound signals. When Sniffy is switched to standard extinction, the magazine sound no longer occurs. Without the magazine sound to "call" him from the bar, Sniffy can do several things. He *may* come down off the bar and sniff the food hopper. He *may* also come down off the bar and do something else such as grooming himself or walking around in the operant chamber. However, in the first stages of extinction, the bar-pressing response is still very strong. Thus, the thing that Sniffy is most likely to do is to remain mounted at the bar and continue to press it again and again. Because Sniffy can press the bar faster if he doesn't come down to examine the food hopper after each bar press, his response rate goes up.

A second thing to note about the standard extinction procedure is that the Operant Associations mind window shows that extinction results in the elimination of the bar–sound association and action strength. However, the sound–food association remains intact. The bar–sound association and action strength dissipate because the bar presses no longer produce the sound. The sound–food association remains intact because Sniffy never hears the sound without receiving a food pellet.

Exercise 8: Secondary Reinforcement

To get Sniffy to bar-press in the first place, you did two things. During magazine training, you turned the magazine sound into a secondary reinforcer by pairing it with food. Then during shaping, you strengthened an association between the bar and the sound. Finally, during standard extinction, you turned off both the sound and the food. In this exercise, you will demonstrate the reinforcing power of the magazine sound by leaving it turned on during extinction. In other words, you will set up an extinction experiment in which Sniffy no longer receives any food when he presses the bar. However, bar presses will continue to produce the magazine sound (as if the magazine continued to operate when it contained no food pellets). Presenting the magazine sound as a consequence of bar pressing during extinction will have two effects. First, presenting the sound after each bar press during extinction will for a while continue to reinforce bar presses, with the result that the extinction process will be slowed down. Second, because the sound occurs but no food pellets are delivered, the sound–food association will eventually dissipate.

To set up the experiment, you should follow these steps:

- If the Sniffy Lite program is not running, start it.
- Use the Open command under the File menu to open the file containing the Sniffy that you trained to bar-press for continuous reinforcement in Exercise 5. (This is the file called Ex5 ShapeBP if you followed our file-naming suggestion.)
- Use the Save As command to save the file under an appropriate new name (such as Ex8 SecRef) in the Sniffy Files folder on your computer's hard drive. *This step is quite important because it preserves your original trained Sniffy file for future use.* You will need your trained Sniffy for future exercises.
- Choose the Design Operant Conditioning Experiment command from the Experiment menu.

- When the dialog box opens, point the cursor at the button labeled "Extinction" and click your left mouse button to select that option.
- Point the cursor at the box next to Mute Pellet Dispenser and click it to uncheck this option. Setting up extinction with Mute Pellet Dispenser turned off means that Sniffy's bar presses will no longer produce food pellets, but he will continue to hear the magazine sound as a consequence of bar pressing. The primary reinforcer (food) is turned off, but the secondary reinforcer (the magazine sound) remains on.
- After checking to be sure that you have made the correct setting, click the OK command button.
- After you click OK, the dialog box will disappear and the Sniffy Lite program will begin running again. Immediately after clicking OK, your cumulative record will look something like that shown here:

- If you want to speed up the experiment, select the Isolate Sniffy (Accelerate Time) command from the Experiment menu.
- Note that the Sniffy Lite program marks the cumulative record to show the point at which extinction starts and informs you that the magazine is not muted.

Because Sniffy hears the magazine sound after each bar press, we no longer see the extinction burst, the initial increase in the rate of bar pressing, that we saw during standard extinction without the magazine sound. Each time he hears the magazine sound, Sniffy comes down off the bar and sniffs at the food hopper.

Your extinction criterion is a 5-minute period during which Sniffy presses the bar no more than twice. When that point is reached, you should:

- Save your Secondary Reinforcement file.

When the extinction criterion is reached, you should estimate the number of responses that Sniffy made between the onset of extinction and the time when the criterion was reached, as well as the time required to reach the extinction criterion.

Compare Sniffy's extinction with the magazine sound turned on with the extinction that you observed in the previous exercise. This comparison will reveal that Sniffy makes more responses and that the extinction process takes more time when the magazine sound remains on than when it is muted. This difference is caused by the initial secondary reinforcing power of the magazine sound when it occurs during extinction.

Finally, note that after extinction with the magazine sound turned on, the sound–food association extinguished, but the bar–sound association did not. The sound–food association dissipates because the sound occurs but no food pellet is presented. The bar–sound association remains intact because Sniffy continues to hear the sound after each bar press.

Exercise 9: Spontaneous Recovery

A single extinction session is not enough to reduce permanently the frequency of an operant response to its pretraining frequency. If an animal that has apparently been fully extinguished is removed from the operant chamber, allowed to rest in its home cage for 24 hours, and then returned to the operant chamber for a second extinction session, its response rate at the start of the second session will be greater than it was at the end of the first extinction session. This rest-produced reappearance of an extinguished operant response is called **spontaneous recovery**.

To simulate the phenomenon with Sniffy:

- Open a file in which Sniffy has been trained to press the bar and then extinguished. Either your Ex7 Ext or your Ex8 SecRef file will work for this purpose.
- Use the Save As command to save the file under a new appropriate name (such as Ex9 SponRec) in the Sniffy Files folder on your computer's hard drive.

- Choose Remove Sniffy for Time-Out from the Experiment menu. To simulate taking a rest, Sniffy will disappear momentarily and then reappear.
- When he reappears, his bar-pressing rate will be higher than it was at the end of extinction, but lower than it was before extinction. Immediately after the time-out, your cumulative record should resemble that shown below:

- If you want to speed up the experiment, select the Isolate Sniffy (Accelerate Time) command from the Experiment menu.
- Check the Operant Associations mind window shortly after starting your spontaneous recovery experiment. You'll recall that standard extinction (with the magazine sound muted) produces extinction of the bar–sound association and action strength, whereas extinction with the magazine sound not muted causes extinction of the sound–food association. At the beginning of the spontaneous recovery experiment, the extinguished items are partly restored. This partial reappearance of the extinguished items is the "psychological" reason why Sniffy presses the bar more often at the beginning of the second extinction session than he did at the end of the first extinction session.
- Let the Sniffy Lite program run until Sniffy meets the extinction criterion again.
- Compare the number of responses made and the time required to reach the extinction criterion during this second extinction session with the number of responses and time required during the first extinction session. This comparison will reveal that the second time around Sniffy makes fewer responses and takes less time to reach the criterion.

Some Questions and Things to Do

Behavioral Repertoire

The items in the behavioral repertoire of an untrained Sniffy can be categorized into roughly eight major components:

- *Paw lifting:* Sniffy lifts his front paws off the floor anywhere in the operant chamber. Do not include bar pressing in this category.
- *Face touching:* Sniffy touches his face with one of his front paws.
- *Head lowering:* Sniffy lowers his head down between his back legs as if he were licking his genitals.
- *Sniffing:* Sniffy stands with all four paws on the floor and twitches his whiskers. You can see his whiskers twitch when he is either facing toward you or toward the left or right walls of the operant chamber. When he is facing the back wall, you can't see his whiskers, but you can see him wiggling a bit.
- *Locomotion:* Sniffy walks around or turns his body.
- *Bar pressing:* Sniffy presses the bar.
- *Hopper sniffing and eating:* Sniffy sticks his head into the food hopper. If a foot pellet is there, he eats it.
- *Drinking:* Sniffy places his mouth against the side or end of the drinking spout and makes licking movements (similar to sniffs).

Training Sniffy to press the bar modifies the frequencies with which he performs many of the behaviors in his behavior repertoire. To determine how the frequencies are changed, first watch a completely untrained Sniffy for 15 minutes and record how frequently he performs each kind of behavior. (To produce a completely untrained Sniffy, simply open a new file.) Then watch and record the behavior of the completely trained Sniffy that you produced in Exercise 5 for the same length of time.

1. How much more often in comparison to the untrained Sniffy does the trained Sniffy press the bar?
2. Which categories of behavior occur less often in the trained Sniffy?
3. Are any categories of behavior unchanged?
4. Do any categories other than bar pressing increase in frequency?

A major component of this exercise is figuring out how to set things up so that you can accurately and objectively record the frequencies with which Sniffy performs the various categories of behavior. It is a good idea to work with a partner, where one person watches Sniffy continuously and calls out the behaviors as they occur while the other person enters the data on paper.

Another Effect of Magazine Training

If left entirely to his own devices in an operant chamber that has been programmed to deliver a food pellet each time the bar is pressed, Sniffy will train himself to press the bar. To find out how long it takes a completely naïve Sniffy to train himself to press the bar, open a new file, set up the program to deliver a food pellet for each bar press, hide Sniffy to accelerate time, and keep an eye on the Operant Associations mind window. When the Lab Assistant says that Sniffy is fully trained, mark the cumulative record (by choosing Mark Record from the Experiment menu). Repeat the process with the magazine-trained Sniffy that you produced in Exercise 4. Compare the times that the completely naïve Sniffy and the magazine-trained Sniffy require to complete their self-training. The magazine-trained Sniffy should self-train faster. Why?

6

Schedules of Reinforcement and the Partial-Reinforcement Effect

Background and Examples

In extinction, reinforcement is completely cut off. This action simulates the situation in which a once available food source has ceased to exist. Another even more common real-world scenario is one in which a response is sometimes reinforced and sometimes not reinforced. When a wild rat searches for food, there is no guarantee it will find food in the same place every time. The rat's searches are based on the probability of locating food. Going to a location where there once was food and finding none would not necessarily discourage the rat from trying there again at some other time when food might be available.

In a similar way, consider what your reaction might be if you turned on a light switch and the light failed to come on. How you would react would likely depend on your previous experience with that light switch. If the switch had worked reliably in the past, you would probably immediately go to look for a new light bulb. However, if the switch had sometimes required several flicks before the light came on, you would probably spend some time flicking it on and off before you decided that this time the problem was likely a burnt-out bulb.

With regard to Sniffy, so far we have discussed reinforcement as something that occurs either every time Sniffy presses the bar or not at all. However, you can also choose to reinforce only some of Sniffy's bar presses. The technical name for reinforcing every instance of a target behavior is **continuous reinforcement (CRF)**. The technical term for reinforcing some, but not all, instances of a behavior is **partial reinforcement (PRF)**. A rule that determines which instances of a response to reinforce is called a **schedule of reinforcement**. PRF schedules affect the temporal patterning of responses as viewed on a cumulative record. In addition, PRF schedules enhance resistance to extinction. By enhanced resistance to extinction, we mean that, if a response has been reinforced on a PRF schedule, the animal will make more responses during extinction than would be the case if the response had always been reinforced (continuous reinforcement).

The comparative effects of partial and continuous reinforcement on resistance to extinction can have real-life implications. Suppose that you are a parent of a young child. Many children who are about 2 years old develop a tendency to exhibit temper tantrums. In fact, this problem is so common that children in that age group are sometimes called the "terrible twos." How parents react to tantrums can have a profound influence on the duration of this phase of their child's development.

When a child has a tantrum, you can either reinforce the tantrum behavior by giving the child what he or she wants or not reinforce the behavior by letting the child kick and scream until he or she gets tired and stops. (We assume you are not a person who would spank a child for tantrum behavior.) The best advice to parents of children who are just beginning to have tantrums is never to reinforce the behavior. If you never reinforce a tantrum, your child should pass through this phase quickly. However, many parents end up giving in to the child, especially if a tantrum occurs in public. The findings of operant conditioning suggest that if you are going to reinforce the behavior, it is better to do so consistently. That way, when the time comes to extinguish the behavior, the process should be faster than if you sometimes let the child scream and sometimes give the child what he or she wants.

Continuous reinforcement is the most efficient way to shape a new behavior quickly. But once the target behavior has been conditioned, continuous reinforcement is no longer necessary. Imagine the nursery-school teacher's task with a new class of children. There are a great many new things the students need to learn—not only the prescribed lessons, but also social skills that will allow them to participate in the classroom. In the beginning, the teacher needs to reinforce the children's appropriate behaviors as often as possible. The teacher dispenses praise, stickers, and certificates and stamps stars on their hands. The nursery school teacher is a dispenser of reinforcers who at first must provide as close to a continuous-reinforcement schedule as is possible. However, this level of reinforcement is impossible to maintain, and children are soon exposed to a partial-reinforcement schedule. In first grade, children who know an answer to a question are expected to raise their hands and wait to be called on, and not every raised hand is recognized. As long as each child gets occasional recognition, the skills that they have learned will not disappear because, with partial reinforcement, it is difficult to extinguish their learned behaviors.

As noted, a schedule of reinforcement is a rule for determining which responses to reinforce. In their book *Schedules of Reinforcement*, C. B. Ferster and B. F. Skinner (1957) describe many different possible schedules. However, all the described schedules are made of combinations of two basic "families" of schedules: **ratio schedules** and **interval schedules**.

Ratio schedules reinforce the subject for making some particular number of responses. On a **fixed-ratio (FR) schedule**, the number of responses required is always the same. On an FR-5 schedule, the subject must make five responses for each reinforcement. This is rather like being paid for piecework, where the amount of money earned depends on the amount of work accomplished according to a prearranged pay scale. Because the amount of money earned is directly proportional to the amount of work performed, piecework tends to produce high rates of output.

When we observe animals on an FR schedule in the operant chamber, the pattern of performance seen on the cumulative record depends on the size of the ratio. Small FR schedules, which require only a small number of responses for each reinforcement, produce fast, steady responding. However, the performance of an animal that is being maintained on a large FR schedule is characterized by a pause after the receipt of each reinforcement, followed by an abrupt transition to rapid, steady responding until the next reinforcement occurs. As the size of a large FR schedule is increased, the pause after each reinforcement becomes longer. We can see something that resembles this pattern of responding in the behavior of a student who finds it difficult to start the next task after finishing a major assignment. The student's behavior is affected by the fact that a lot more work is required before the next reinforcement is obtained.

On a **variable-ratio (VR) schedule**, the value of the schedule specifies an average number of responses required to obtain reinforcement, but the exact number of responses varies from reinforcement to reinforcement. On a VR-5 schedule, the subject must make 5 responses on average for each reinforcement. Sometimes the subject must make 8 or 10 responses before reinforcement occurs, but these large values are balanced by occasions when reinforcement occurs after only 1 or 2 responses. VR schedules typically produce high rates of responding with no long pauses.

VR schedules are common in everyday life. Las Vegas–style slot machines pay off on a VR schedule, as does trying to arrange a date for Saturday night, or selling something on a commission basis. In all these situations, there is some chance or probability of success associated with every "response" that you make. The more often you respond, the more often you will be reinforced.

Interval schedules reinforce the subject for the first response made after a specified time interval has elapsed since the last reinforcement was received. The time period during which reinforcement is unavailable begins when the subject receives a reinforcer. The interval thus specifies a minimum amount of time that must elapse between reinforced responses. On a **fixed-interval (FI) schedule**, the interval that must elapse before another response will be reinforced is always the same. On an FI-60 second schedule, exactly 60 seconds must always elapse after the receipt of one reinforcer before another response will be reinforced.

If your school is typical, every class period ends at a specified time. If you observe your fellow students, you will notice that their behavior changes as the time when the class is scheduled to end approaches. Early in the class period, everyone listens fairly attentively, and many students busily take notes. However, as the end of class approaches, students begin to put their notes away and prepare to leave.

On a **variable-interval (VI) schedule**, the time interval following reinforcement that must elapse before the next response is reinforced varies from reinforcement to reinforcement. On a VI-10 second schedule, the time interval would average 10 seconds. Few, if any, real-life situations are exactly equivalent to VI scheduling in the laboratory. However, trying to telephone someone whose line is frequently busy is similar to reinforcement on a VI schedule. Your call won't go through until the line is free, and the line is busy for varying periods. The difference is that on a pure VI schedule, once the time interval has elapsed, the reinforcer becomes available and remains available until the subject responds, but when you are trying to call an often busy telephone number, the line is busy and free intermittently. You can miss chances to complete the call by not trying often enough.

Each of these simple schedules produces a characteristic performance from subjects maintained on the schedule long enough for their behavior to stabilize. Depending on which schedule is involved, the animal may press the bar at a steady, predictable rate, or its response rate may vary in predictable ways. Prior to the appearance of the characteristic pattern of responding associated with the schedule, there is a period of acquisition during which the animal gradually adjusts to the schedule.

Variable-Ratio (VR) and Variable-Interval (VI) Schedules

Both VR and VI schedules produce steady responding, but at different rates. VR schedules produce fast, steady responding; VI schedules produce slow, steady responding.

The difference between the performances maintained by VR and VI schedules is nicely illustrated in an experiment described by Reynolds (1975). The experiment involved two pigeons pecking at disks for food reinforcement in separate operant chambers. The experiment involved a **yoked experimental design**, which means that the behavior of the first pigeon could affect the other bird's reinforcement schedule. In the first chamber, pigeon A's disk pecking was reinforced on a VR schedule that the experimenter had programmed. In the other, completely isolated chamber, pigeon B's disk pecking was reinforced on a VI schedule in which the values of the intervals were determined by pigeon A's behavior. Each time pigeon A received a reinforcer for completing a ratio, a reinforcer became available for pigeon B's next response.

Idealized performances of two pigeons in yoked operant chambers. Both birds peck steadily. However, although both birds receive the same number of reinforcements almost simultaneously, the VR bird makes many more responses.

The graph shows hypothetical cumulative records generated by two birds in this kind of experiment. Note that both birds respond at a nearly constant rate, but the bird on the VR schedule responds faster than the bird on the VI schedule. Although both birds' pecking behaviors are reinforced at virtually the same instant and although both always receive the same amount of reinforcement, there is a distinct difference in the rate at which they peck. This difference is caused by differences in the way in which the schedules interact with the birds' pecking behavior.

Fixed Ratio (FR) Schedules

As shown in the next graph, the typical FR performance depends on the size of the ratio—that is, on the fixed number of responses required for each reinforcement. What constitutes a small ratio depends on the organism and the effort required in making the response. For Sniffy and other rats pressing a bar, a small ratio is anything requiring up to 20 bar presses. For a pigeon pecking an illuminated disk, a small ratio is anything up to about 50. With small ratios, the performance is quite steady with no pause after each reinforcement. With large ratios, there is a pause after each reinforcement, followed by an abrupt transition to a high, stable rate until the next reinforcer is received.

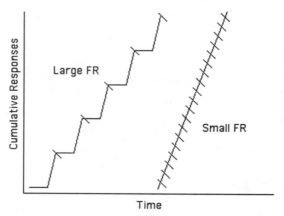

Idealized performances maintained by large and small FR schedules.

Fixed-Interval (FI) Schedules

Overall, FI schedules maintain rather slow rates of responding, more or less comparable to those maintained by VI schedules. However, whereas the VI performance is steady, the typical FI performance involves a pause after the receipt of each reinforcement, followed by a gradually accelerating response rate until the subject is responding moderately fast just before the next reinforcement is due. This typical FI response pattern, an idealized version of which is depicted in the next graph, is often called the **FI scallop**. As is the case with FR schedules, the pauses that occur after the receipt of a reinforcer are much more pronounced on large FI schedules than on small FI schedules.

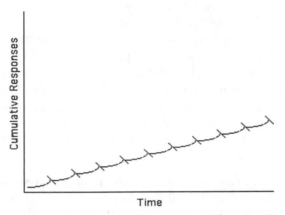

Idealized performance maintained by an FI schedule.

Setting Up a Schedule in the Design Operant Conditioning Experiment Dialog Box

Let's consider how to set up schedule experiments in Sniffy Lite. You establish different reinforcement schedules by choosing the Design Operant Conditioning Experiment command from the Experiment menu. When you execute this command, the following dialog box appears:

When you are programming reinforcement schedules, you work with the left part of the dialog box under Reinforcement Schedule. Here is how the Reinforcement Schedule section of the dialog box works:

- The Fixed and Variable alternatives at the far left determine whether the schedule requirements will be fixed or variable.
- The buttons labeled Responses and Seconds determine whether Sniffy is on a ratio or interval schedule.
- Choosing Responses sets up a ratio schedule.
- Choosing Seconds sets up an interval schedule.
- You set the value of the schedule (the number of responses required or the number of seconds after a reinforcement before another response can be reinforced) by typing a number into the text box. For example, if you wanted to set up a VI-20 second schedule, you would select the Variable and Seconds alternatives and type 20 in the text box.

Sniffy can be trained to bar-press on schedules with very large values (for example, VR-250 or FI-120). However, you need to approach large schedule values gradually. In the following exercises, you will train Sniffy to bar-press on VR, VI, FR, and FI schedules with values of 50. This task can be accomplished easily if you approach the value of 50 by first training Sniffy to respond on schedules with a value of 5 and then go through the intermediate values of 10, 20, and 35.

When you first place Sniffy on a reinforcement schedule and each time you increase the value of the schedule, the bar–sound association and action strength will start to go down. In other words, Sniffy will start to extinguish. However, if he was fully enough trained before the change and if the increase in the schedule value isn't too large, the bar–sound association and action strength will bottom out well above their minimum values and start to increase again after a while. Wait until they reach or very closely approach their maximum levels before again increasing the value of the schedule.

- Selecting the button labeled "Continuous" sets up continuous reinforcement. All Sniffy's bar presses are reinforced. This setting is the default in effect when you first select a target behavior for the program to reinforce automatically.
- Selecting the button labeled "Extinction" sets up an extinction condition.
- When you click the OK button after setting up a reinforcement schedule, the dialog box disappears, and the Sniffy Lite program starts reinforcing Sniffy according to the schedule you established.

- When you click Cancel, the dialog box disappears and the program continues reinforcing Sniffy according to whatever schedule was in effect before you opened the dialog box. None of the settings that you made while the dialog box was open are implemented.

Exercise 10: Placing Sniffy on a Small VR Schedule

Here are the steps that you should follow to place Sniffy on a small variable-ratio (VR) schedule of reinforcement. Except for the settings in the Design Operant Conditioning Experiment dialog box, you would follow the same steps to place Sniffy on any small-value schedule.

- Before Sniffy can be placed on a schedule, he must first be fully trained to press the bar for continuous reinforcement.
  - If you still have the file that you created after first training Sniffy to press the bar in Exercise 5 (the file that we suggested you name Ex5 ShapeBP), use the Open command in the File menu to open the file.
  - If you do not have your original trained Sniffy file, you can use the file named ShapeBP that is located in the Sample Files folder.
- Look at the Operant Associations mind window. (If necessary, make the Operant Associations window visible by selecting it from the Mind Windows section of the Windows menu.) Make sure that the sound–food association, bar–sound association, and action strength are at or very near their maximum levels. If you have opened your own file and discover that any of these measures is below its maximum level, you can let the program run until they reach their maximums before going on to the next step.
- Select the Save As command from the File menu to give the file an appropriate new name and save it in the Sniffy Files folder on your computer's hard drive. *This step is important because it preserves your original CRF-trained Sniffy for use in other experiments.* Because in this example we will be creating a file in which Sniffy is trained to respond on a VR-5 schedule, we suggest that you call the new file Ex10-VR5.
- Choose the Design Operant Conditioning Experiments command from the Experiment menu. Under Reinforcement

Schedule, select the Variable and Responses alternatives. Type 5 in the text box. Click OK.
- If you want to speed up the experiment, select the Isolate Sniffy (Accelerate Time) command from the Experiment menu.

Shortly after the Design Operant Conditioning Experiment dialog box closes, your Cumulative Record window will look something like the following. Note that the Sniffy Lite program marks the point at which the VR-5 schedule was introduced.

Immediately after being switched onto a schedule, when Sniffy encounters unreinforced responding for the first time, he will begin to extinguish. The Operant Associations mind window will display this process as a decrease in the strength of the bar–sound association and action strength. If Sniffy is fully trained on continuous reinforcement before you place him on a VR-5 schedule, he will not extinguish fully. However, if his continuous reinforcement training is incomplete, or if you try to place him on a schedule with too large an initial value (such as VR-25), he will extinguish.

If Sniffy is going to adjust successfully to the schedule on which you have placed him, the bar–sound association and action strength will begin to increase again after Sniffy has received several reinforcements on the schedule.

Sniffy is completely trained on the schedule when the bar–sound association and action strength approach their maximum values. At that point, Sniffy's cumulative record will be displaying the response pattern typical of the schedule on which Sniffy is being maintained.

- When you are satisfied that Sniffy's training is sufficient, choose the Save command from the File menu to save your file.

Exercise 11: Increasing the Value of Sniffy's VR Schedule

Sniffy can be trained to respond on schedules with quite high values (such as VR-100 or FI-60 sec) provided these high values are approached gradually through intermediate stages. Here are the steps to increase the value of a schedule. As an illustration, we will assume that you are going to increase the value of the VR-5 schedule from the previous exercise.

- If the Sniffy Lite program is not running, start it.
- Use the Open command under the File menu to open your VR-5 file from Exercise 10.
- Check the Operant Associations mind window to be sure that the bar–sound association and action strength are at or near their maximum levels. If not, let the program run longer.
- Select the Save As command from the File menu and save the file under an appropriate name in the Sniffy Files folder on your computer's hard drive. Because we are going to be increasing the value of Sniffy's VR-5 schedule to VR-10, we suggest that you call the new file Ex11-VR10. Saving the new file under a different name preserves your original VR-5 file for future use if the need arises.
- Select the Design Operant Conditioning Experiment command from the Experiment menu. Be sure that the Variable and Responses alternatives are selected, type the number 10 in the text box, and click OK.
- If you want to speed up the experiment, select the Isolate Sniffy (Accelerate Time) command from the Experiment menu.
- Because Sniffy is now experiencing longer runs of unreinforced trials, the bar–sound association and action strength will weaken at first. However, after Sniffy has received several reinforcements on the new schedule, these values will start going back up. When they approach their maxima again, choose the Save command from the File menu to preserve your VR-10 trained Sniffy.

Repeat relevant parts of these instructions to shape Sniffy up to a VR-50 schedule. Sniffy will easily and quickly reach the VR-50 endpoint if you use VR-20 and VR-35 as your intermediate steps. If you like to "live dangerously," try stepping Sniffy up to a VR-50 after VR-10 or VR-20. He may or may not extinguish with larger steps.

The cumulative record that you obtain once Sniffy has fully adapted to the VR-50 schedule should resemble the following graph. Note the rapid, reasonably steady response pattern.

Exercise 12: Variable-Interval Schedules

Follow the generalized instructions given in the section titled "Setting Up a Schedule in the Design Operant Conditioning Experiment Dialog Box" (page 79) to shape Sniffy up to a VI-50 second schedule.

If you want to speed up the experiment, select the Isolate Sniffy (Accelerate Time) command from the Experiment menu.

The cumulative record that you obtain once Sniffy has fully adapted to the VI-50 schedule should resemble the following graph. Note the slow, reasonably steady response pattern.

Exercise 13: Fixed-Ratio Schedules

Follow the generalized instructions given in the section "Setting Up a Schedule in the Design Operant Conditioning Experiment Dialog Box" (page 79) to shape Sniffy up to an FR-50 schedule.

If you want to speed up the experiment, select the Isolate Sniffy (Accelerate Time) command from the Experiment menu.

The cumulative record that you obtain once Sniffy has fully adapted to the FR-50 schedule should resemble the following graph. Note the pauses in responding that occur after each reinforcement is received and the abrupt transitions to rapid responding at the end of each pause.

Exercise 14: Fixed Interval Schedules

Follow the generalized instructions given in the section titled "Setting Up a Schedule in the Design Operant Conditioning Experiment Dialog Box" (page 79) to shape Sniffy up to an FI-50 second schedule.

If you want to speed up the experiment, select the Isolate Sniffy (Accelerate Time) command from the Experiment menu.

The cumulative record that you obtain once Sniffy has fully adapted to the FI-50 schedule should resemble the following graph. Note the pauses after each reinforcement is received, followed by rather gradual transitions to moderate response rates shortly before the next reinforcement is due to occur.

How Realistic Are Sniffy's Schedule Performances?

The speed with which Sniffy adapts to reinforcement schedules is one of the places where we sacrificed realism for convenience. Real rats adapt to schedules and changes in schedules quite slowly. In many instances, a real rat requires several daily 1-hour training sessions before its pattern of responding in the cumulative record begins to resemble the response pattern that a particular schedule "typically" produces. Sniffy adapts to schedules and schedule changes much faster. We speeded up Sniffy's learning process so that you will have the opportunity to look at the effects of many different schedules in a reasonable amount of time.

Sniffy's schedule performances are not perfect replicas of the idealized performances shown in the first part of this chapter and in many textbooks on the psychology of learning. Idealized performances are designed to communicate ideas about what psychologists think schedule performances would look like if all the "noise" could be averaged out. The actual performances that you obtain with Sniffy and the actual performances of real rats are rarely ideal, because the factors that tend to produce ideal performances are not the only things determining the animal's behavior. For example, VR schedules are supposed to produce rapid, steady responding, and they tend to do so. However, pressing the bar is not the only thing that rats do while being reinforced on a VR schedule. Sometimes they take drinks of water. Sometimes they groom or scratch themselves. Sometimes they wander around the operant chamber for a little while. All these interruptions make actual VR performances less rapid and especially less steady than they would be if the only factors involved were those discussed in the first parts of this chapter.

Thus the fact that Sniffy's cumulative records are not perfect replicas of ideal schedule performances means that, to a degree, Sniffy is behaving like a real rat. If you look at reproductions of the actual performances of real rats in scientific journal articles and in specialized books on reinforcement schedules, you will discover that Sniffy's schedule performances fall within the range of performances that real rats sometimes produce.

Exercise 15: The Effect of Partial Reinforcement on Extinction

Partial reinforcement dramatically increases a response's resistance to extinction. Animals whose responding has been maintained by a partial-reinforcement schedule make many more responses during extinction than do animals whose responding has been maintained on continuous reinforcement. In addition, ratio schedules tend to produce greater resistance to extinction than interval schedules, and variable schedules tend to produce greater resistance to extinction than fixed schedules. The Sniffy Lite program enables you to observe these differences in resistance to extinction. To measure Sniffy's resistance to extinction following partial reinforcement, you should follow these steps:

- Open a Sniffy Lite file in which Sniffy has been fully trained to respond on a moderate- or large-value schedule. We suggest you use a file in which you have trained Sniffy to respond on a schedule with a value of at least 25 (that is,VR-25, FR-25, VI-25 sec, or FI-25 sec).
- Look at the Operant Associations mind window to verify that the bar–sound association is at or near its maximum level.
- Save the file under an appropriate new name (such as Ex14-VR25Ext) to preserve your original schedule file for future use.
- Choose the Design Operant Conditioning Experiment command from the Experiment menu.
- Click the Extinction option in the dialog box, make sure there is a check mark in the box next to Mute Pellet Dispenser, and click the OK command button.
- If you want to speed up the experiment, select the Isolate Sniffy (Accelerate Time) command from the Experiment menu.
- Let the program run until Sniffy reaches the extinction criterion of no more than two responses during a 5-minute period.
- Save the file.
- Print the cumulative record and determine how many responses Sniffy made and how much time elapsed before he reached the extinction criterion.
- Compare your partial-reinforcement extinction results with the extinction results that you obtained earlier when Sniffy's responding had been maintained by continuous reinforcement.

Some Questions and Things to Do

The exercises in this chapter barely scratch the surface of what it is possible to do with schedules of reinforcement.

Does Schedule Size Affect Overall Response Rate?

On an interval schedule, the schedule's "size" is the number of seconds after reinforcement before the next reinforcement becomes available. On a ratio schedule, the schedule's "size" is the number of responses required for a reinforcement. Exercises 11, 12, 13, and 14 ask you to set up, respectively, VR, VI, FR, and FI schedules of "size" 50.

Manipulating schedule size should have different effects for different schedule types. Pick a couple of different schedule types, such as VI and VR. Fully train Sniffy (so that the bar–sound association and action strength approach their maxima) to respond to values of 5, 10, 25, 50, and 100 for each of the two schedule types. Then determine the number of times he presses the bar during 30 minutes of program time and divide that number by 30 to obtain an average number of responses per minute.

- How does the response rate change as the value of the schedules increases?
- Does it change in the same way for the two kinds of schedules?

Does Schedule Size Affect Resistance to Extinction?

Pick a schedule type (VR, VI, FR, or FI) and fully train Sniffy (so that the bar–sound association is at or very close to its maximum value) to respond to values of 5, 10, 25, 50, and 100. Then determine how many responses Sniffy will make and how much time passes before bar pressing extinguishes with schedules of different values.

- How does the value of a schedule affect response rate?
- How does the value of the schedule affect resistance to extinction?

7

Shaping Behaviors Other Than Bar Pressing

If you have ever watched circus animals performing, you will likely have seen the animals do a variety of "amazing" things that untrained animals of the same species do not do—things like bears riding bicycles or dogs walking tight ropes. Or you may have visited a roadside attraction such as the I.Q. Zoo in Hot Springs, Arkansas, where chickens jump through hoops and play baseball and a duck plays the piano. One of the most important techniques that animal trainers employ to get animals to do these unusual things is shaping. To give you additional experience with shaping and to provide a bit of fun, we have enabled you to shape Sniffy to perform some interesting behaviors.

Shaping a live animal involves a number of steps. The first step is to establish a secondary reinforcer through a procedure resembling magazine training. The secondary reinforcer must be a stimulus whose timing you can precisely control. A common procedure used with dogs and many other kinds of animals is called "clicker training." You get a little noisemaker and teach the animal that, whenever it hears the clicker sound, you will give it a small treat.

Before beginning to shape an animal, many trainers set up a **shaping hierarchy**, a sequence of behaviors that progressively resemble the target behavior more and more closely. At the bottom of the hierarchy is a behavior that (the trainer hopes) the animal will perform spontaneously and that resembles the target behavior in some way. When the animal performs this first behavior, the trainer starts out by reinforcing that behavior whenever it occurs. As a consequence, the animal will begin to perform the first-step behavior more frequently.

Animals do not always do things in exactly the same way. Their behavior is variable. Eventually, the animal will do something that resembles the target behavior more closely than was the case with the first item in hierarchy. At that point, the trainer reinforces the second-step behavior and requires the animal to repeat that behavior to obtain further reinforcements.

If the trainer is skilful and persistent enough, the process of reinforcing behaviors that resemble the target behavior more and more closely will eventually lead the animal to perform a target behavior that an untrained member of its species would never perform spontaneously and that is spectacular looking enough to be impressive.

The exercises in this chapter will not make you into an expert animal trainer. However, they will provide you with practice in taking Sniffy through short shaping hierarchies that culminate in behaviors that are fun to watch. The target behaviors that you can train Sniffy to perform are:

- Beg
- Roll (that is, turn a somersault)
- Face wipe

To ensure that you succeed in shaping Sniffy to perform these behaviors if you try, we have provided lots of unrealistic help. The Sniffy Lite program will automatically record and reinforce target behaviors even though the behaviors do not involve interacting with a device in a way that would permit automatic recording with a live animal. And if you have trouble figuring out what to do, you can get help from the Shaping Tutor, which can be set to record and reinforce precursor behaviors for each of the target behaviors.

Disclaimer: *The exercises in this chapter do not provide a realistic preview of what you can expect if you ever try to shape a live animal.*

- To train Sniffy to roll or face wipe, you begin by reinforcing grooming movements with a sound associated with food. Yet, research with several kinds of mammals has shown that presenting food or secondary reinforcers associated with food is not an effective way of increasing the frequency of grooming movements (for example, Shettleworth, 1975).
- Reinforcing a precursor behavior will cause Sniffy to start doing something else that is qualitatively different from (and we think more interesting than) the precursor behavior. In contrast, shaping a real animal ordinarily involves leading the animal through a large number of small quantitative changes that add up to a major change in behavior only after a protracted program of training.

Nevertheless, we believe that practicing with these simple examples will help you learn the *principles* of shaping. Just don't expect a real animal to be as "cooperative" as Sniffy.

Exercise 16: Shaping Sniffy to Beg

To see what the behavior that we call begging looks like, open the file entitled BegDemo, which is located in the Sample Files folder. Follow these steps to train Sniffy to beg:

- Open the file from Exercise 4 that we suggested you call "Ex4 MagTrain."
- Select the Save As command from the File menu to give the file an appropriate new name (such as Ex16 ShapeBeg) and save it in the Sniffy Files folder on your computer's hard drive. *Saving the file with a new name before you start shaping Sniffy preserves your original magazine-training file for future use.* If your first attempt at shaping is unsuccessful, you can go back and try again without having to magazine-train Sniffy again.
- If the latest Cumulative Record is not visible, make it visible by selecting it from the Cumulative Record section of the Windows menu.
- Select the Design Operant Conditioning Experiment command from the Experiment menu.
- In the dialog box that appears, select Beg from the Target Behavior section of the Reinforcement Action drop-down menu. After making the selection, click on OK to close the dialog box.
- Note that the terms CRF and Beg appear in the cumulative record. This notation means that the program will automatically reinforce every instance of begging and that the cumulative record will record begging movements.
- As your first approximation to begging, give Sniffy a pellet of food whenever he rears up facing forward (that is, facing you) anywhere in the operant chamber.
- After you have reinforced rearing up facing forward a number of times, you will begin to see instances of begging; and the program will automatically reinforce these.

- If you are patient, the time will come when Sniffy will beg 10 or more times during a 5-minute interval. At that point, you can stop shaping, sit back, and watch the progressive effect of reinforcement as Sniffy continues to beg more and more frequently.
- Sniffy is fully trained when the Action Strength column in the Operant Associations mind window approaches its maximum with Beg as the automatically reinforced behavior. At that point, select the Save command from the File menu to preserve your trained Sniffy for future use.

If You Have Trouble

For users who encounter difficulty with shaping, we have provided a section of the Reinforcement Action menu in the Design Operant Conditioning dialog box called the **Shaping Tutor**.

After 45 to 60 minutes of attempting to shape Sniffy according to the instructions just given, Sniffy should be begging *at least* 10 times during each 5-minute interval, delineated by the alternating solid and dotted vertical lines in the cumulative record. If your attempt at shaping fails to obtain that minimum result, something is wrong.

One possibility is that Sniffy has not been properly magazine trained. Look at the Operant Associations mind window. The Sound–Food association level should be at its maximum on the scale. If it isn't, either go back and repeat Exercise 4 to create a properly magazine-trained Sniffy or use the file entitled MagTrain from the Sniffy Lite CD.

A second possibility is that you may not be reinforcing instances of rearing up toward the front wall as outlined earlier, or not reinforcing these behaviors quickly enough. If you are having trouble reinforcing Sniffy's rearing behaviors:

- Choose the Design Operant Conditioning Experiment command from the Experiment menu.
- Under the Shaping Tutor subsection of the Reinforcement Action menu, choose Rear Up Facing Front.
- The Sniffy Lite program will now automatically reinforce all instances of rearing up facing the front of the cage, including all begs. Watch which actions the program automatically reinforces.

- When you believe that you are capable of effectively reinforcing these behaviors manually, reopen the Design Operant Conditioning Experiment dialog box and choose Beg from the Target Behaviors section of the Reinforcement Action menu.
- If you are unable to reinforce Sniffy effectively by hand, watch what is going on as the program reinforces front-facing rears automatically. Once Sniffy begs 10 or more times in a 5-minute period, reopen the Design Operant Conditioning Experiment dialog box and choose Beg from the Target Behaviors section of the Reinforcement Action menu. The program will complete Sniffy's training automatically.
- When Sniffy is fully trained, save the file.

Exercise 17: Shaping Sniffy to Wipe His Face

To see what Sniffy's face wiping looks like, open the file entitled FaceWipeDemo, which is located in the Sample Files folder of your Sniffy Lite CD. Face Wipe involves Sniffy touching his face with his paw and moving his paw up and down across his eye three times in rapid succession. The precursor behavior for Face Wipe is Face Touch, in which Sniffy touches his face with a paw but does not move his paw up and down across his eye repeatedly. To shape face Wiping, follow these steps:

- Open the file from Exercise 4 that we suggested you call "Ex4 MagTrain."
- Select the Save As command from the File menu to give the file an appropriate new name (such as Ex17 ShapeFaceWipe) and save it in the Sniffy Files folder on your computer's hard drive. *Saving the file with a new name before you start shaping Sniffy preserves your original magazine-training file for future use.*
- If the latest Cumulative Record is not visible, make it visible by selecting it from the Cumulative Record section of the Windows menu.
- If the Operant Associations mind window is not visible, make it visible by selecting it from the Mind Windows section of the Windows menu.

- Select the Design Operant Conditioning Experiment command from the Experiment menu.
- In the dialog box that appears, select Face Wipe from the Target Behavior section of the Reinforcement Action drop-down menu. After making the selection, click on OK to close the dialog box.
- Note that the terms CRF and Face Wipe appear in the cumulative record. These notations mean that the program will automatically reinforce every face wipe and that the cumulative record will record instances of face wiping.
- As your first approximation to face wiping, give Sniffy a pellet of food whenever he touches his face with his paws.
- When Sniffy has been reinforced often enough for touching his face, he will sometimes repeatedly wipe his paw across his eye instead of merely touching his face. This is the behavior we call Face Wipe, and the program will reinforce it automatically whenever it occurs.
- Each time Sniffy performs a face wipe, watch closely what he does after eating the food pellet. He may face wipe again quickly after eating. If he does so, you know you're making progress. Allow him to continue face wiping as long as he will do so. However, if he does something else or touches his face without wiping, continue to reinforce face touching whenever it occurs.
- If you are patient, the time will come when Sniffy will perform a face wipe 8 to 10 times in rapid succession. At that point, you can stop shaping, sit back, and allow the program to automatically reinforce face wiping.
- Sniffy is fully trained when the Action Strength column in the Operant Associations mind window approaches its maximum. At that point, select the Save command from the File menu to preserve your trained Sniffy for future use.

If You Have Trouble

For users who encounter difficulty with shaping, we have provided a section of the Reinforcement Action menu in the Design Operant Conditioning dialog box called the **Shaping Tutor**.

After 30 minutes or so of attempting to shape Sniffy according to the instructions just given, Sniffy should be face wiping *at least* 10 times during each 5-minute interval delineated by the alternating solid and dotted vertical lines in the cumulative record. If your attempt at shaping fails to obtain that minimum result, something is wrong.

One possibility is that Sniffy has not been properly magazine-trained. Look at the Operant Associations mind window. The Sound–Food association level should be at least three-quarters of the way up the scale. If it isn't, either go back and repeat Exercise 4 to create a properly magazine-trained Sniffy or use the file entitled MagTrain from the Sniffy Lite CD.

A second possibility is that you may not be reinforcing instances of face touching as outlined earlier or not reinforcing these behaviors quickly enough. If you are having trouble reinforcing Sniffy's face touching behavior:

- Choose the Design Operant Conditioning Experiment command from the Experiment menu.
- Under the Shaping Tutor subsection of the Reinforcement Action menu, choose Face Touch.
- The Sniffy Lite program will now automatically reinforce all instances of face touching, including all face wipes. Watch which actions the program automatically reinforces.
- When you believe that you are capable of effectively reinforcing these behaviors manually, reopen the Design Operant Conditioning Experiment dialog box and choose Face Wipe from the Target Behaviors section of the Reinforcement Action menu.
- If you are unable to reinforce Sniffy effectively by hand, watch what is going on as the program reinforces face touching and wiping automatically. Once Sniffy face wipes 8 to 10 times in a 1- or 2-minute period, reopen the Design Operant Conditioning Experiment dialog box and choose Face Wipe from the Target Behaviors section of the Reinforcement Action menu. The program will complete Sniffy's training automatically.
- When Sniffy is fully trained, save the file.

Exercise 18: Shaping Sniffy to Roll

The behavior that we call Roll involves Sniffy turning a somersault as he moves from left to right or right to left across the operant chamber. To see what the behavior looks like, open the file called RollDemo, which is located in the Sample Files folder.

Shaping Sniffy to roll involves a shaping hierarchy with two precursor behaviors: head lowering and head tucking. You start out reinforcing instances of head lowering. When the head-lowering movement has been reinforced often enough, head tucks will begin to occur. Head tucking is thus the second item in your shaping hierarchy. Once head tucks are occurring fairly often, you should stop reinforcing head lowering and reinforce head tucks only. Eventually, reinforcing head tucks will begin to produce rolls. Finally, when rolls are occurring reasonably often, you stop reinforcing head tucks and reinforce rolls only. Eventually, Sniffy will have a high probability of rolling whenever he is in a position where he can do so without hitting a wall.

To shape rolling, follow these steps:

- Open the file from Exercise 4 that we suggested you call "Ex4 MagTrain."
- Select the Save As command from the File menu to give the file an appropriate new name (such as Ex18 ShapeRoll) and save it in the Sniffy Files folder on your computer's hard drive. *Saving the file with a new name before you start shaping Sniffy preserves your original magazine-training file for future use.*
- If the latest Cumulative Record is not visible, make it visible by selecting it from the Cumulative Record section of the Windows menu.
- Select the Design Operant Conditioning Experiment command from the Experiment menu.
- In the dialog box that appears, select Roll from the Target Behavior section of the Reinforcement Action drop-down menu. After making the selection, click on OK to close the dialog box.
- Note that the terms CRF and Roll appear in the cumulative record. These notations mean that the program will automatically reinforce every roll and that the cumulative record will record rolls.
- As your first approximation to rolling, give Sniffy a pellet of food when he lowers his head between his hind legs (as if he were licking his genitals).
- When Sniffy has been reinforced often enough for lowering his head, he will sometimes begin to rock back and forth with his head tucked between his hind legs. This is the behavior we call Head Tuck.

- Reinforce all head tucks. At first, also continue to reinforce instances of head lowering. However, when head tucks have become fairly common, stop reinforcing instances of head lowering and reinforce head tucks only.
- When you have reinforced head tucks often enough, you will begin to see the first instances of rolling, and the program will reinforce rolls automatically. At first, continue to reinforce instances of head tucks manually. However, once you have seen a total of about 50 rolls, you can stop reinforcing head tucks. At that point, sit back and allow the program to reinforce rolling automatically.
- When the Action Strength has approached its maximum value with Roll as the automatically reinforced behavior, Sniffy is fully trained. At that point, select the Save command from the File menu to preserve your trained Sniffy for future use.

If You Have Trouble

Shaping Roll from a file in which Sniffy has only been magazine trained should take anywhere from half an hour to an hour. So be patient and don't give up easily. For users who encounter difficulty with shaping, we have provided a section of the Reinforcement Action menu in the Design Operant Conditioning dialog box called the **Shaping Tutor**.

After an hour or so of attempting to shape Sniffy according to the instructions just given, Sniffy should be rolling *at least* two or three times during each 5-minute interval delineated by the alternating solid and dotted vertical lines in the cumulative record.

If your attempt at shaping fails to obtain that minimum result after an hour, something is wrong.

One possibility is that Sniffy has not been properly magazine trained. Look at the Operant Associations mind window. The Sound–Food association level should be at least three-quarters of the way up the scale. If it isn't, either go back and repeat Exercise 4 to created a properly magazine trained Sniffy or use the file entitled MagTrain from the Sniffy Lite CD.

A second possibility is that you may not be reinforcing instances of head lowering and head tucking as outlined earlier, or not reinforcing these behaviors quickly enough. If you are having trouble reinforcing Sniffy's head-lowering and head-tucking behaviors:

- Choose the Design Operant Conditioning Experiment command from the Experiment menu.
- Under the Shaping Tutor subsection of the Reinforcement Action menu, choose Head Lower.
- The Sniffy Lite program will now automatically reinforce all instances of head lowering, including all head tucks and rolls. Watch which actions the program automatically reinforces.
- When you believe that you are capable of effectively reinforcing these behaviors manually, reopen the Design Operant Conditioning Experiment dialog box and choose Roll from the Target Behaviors section of the Reinforcement Action menu.
- If you are unable to reinforce Sniffy effectively by hand, allow the program to train rolling automatically.
- When Sniffy is fully trained, save the file.

Exercise 19: Shaping Sniffy to Perform Other Behaviors

Manually reinforcing any behavior that Sniffy performs spontaneously will have the effect of making that behavior and other similar behaviors occur more frequently. Thus, if you are patient and have good timing, it is possible to train Sniffy to perform a variety of "tricks" other than those that we have documented in this chapter. One family of behaviors is something that we call sniffing. Sniffy sits with his head down near the metal bars that form the floor of the operant chamber and twitches his whiskers. There are four basic examples of this behavior that form a family: sniff to front (Sniffy sniffs while facing you), sniff left and sniff right (Sniffy sniffs with his head pointed toward the left or right side of the chamber), and Sniff rear (Sniffy's back is to you and he wiggles a bit, but his nose is invisible). Reinforcing any one of these behaviors will make the reinforced behavior and the other behaviors in "sniffing family" occur more often. If you consistently reinforce any one of these behaviors and do not reinforce the others, the one that you reinforce will eventually occur much more often than the others. We invite you to explore and discover Sniffy's full repertoire of trainable "tricks."

Exercise 20: Shaping a Cat to Beg or Walk on Its Hind Legs

Limitations in the Sniffy simulation mean there are limits to the variety of things Sniffy can be trained to do. However, animal trainers routinely use shaping to teach real animals to do an enormous variety of things that are physically possible but which an untrained animal would never do. As a simple example, training a physically fit cat to sit up and beg for food and to stand or walk on its hind legs without support is a fairly straightforward process even though untrained cats rarely, if ever, do these things.

Pet food manufacturers produce bite-size cat treats in several flavors, and it is often possible to find a flavor that your cat likes so much that the animal will work to obtain them. In fact, the cat may like them so much that you'll have to keep the treats container locked away to prevent theft. Once you've found your cat's favorite, the treats will constitute a primary reinforcer that you can employ to teach the animal to sit up and beg, to stand and walk on its hind legs, or to do other tricks.

As with Sniffy, the first step in training your cat will be magazine training. You need to find a stimulus that can be delivered with split-second timing when your cat does something right and that can be easily transformed into a secondary reinforcer by pairing it with treat presentation. Stores that sell party supplies often stock a variety of noise makers, and many pet-supply stores sell "clickers" that are designed to provide a sound that can be established as a secondary reinforcer.

You magazine-train a cat in much the same way that you magazine-trained Sniffy. To begin, wait until the cat is near you. Then operate the noisemaker and give the cat a treat. After you have sounded the clicker and given the cat a treat a couple of times with the cat very close by, walk a short distance away before sounding the clicker and giving the cat the next treat. You will know your cat is well magazine-trained when you can call it from anywhere in the house (or neighborhood!) just by sounding the clicker.

Training a cat to sit up and beg or to stand and walk on its hind legs involves requiring the animal to raise its head progressively higher and higher off the ground before you reinforce it by sounding the noisemaker and giving it a treat. Start by watching the cat until it lifts its head somewhat higher than usual. (Standing with its front paws up on something doesn't count.) Then sound the clicker and give the cat a treat. After several reinforcements, the cat will begin walking around with its head held high more often. Because the cat's behavior is variable, sooner or later it will raise its head higher than your first criterion level, and that new higher level then becomes your second approximation that the cat must match to get additional treats. By the time you have reached the third or fourth approximation, the cat will probably be sitting on its hind legs with its front paws off the ground. Once the cat starts to lift its front paws off the ground, it will rather quickly reach a training plateau in which it sits up and "begs" for treats. Depending on your patience, you can either decide that sitting up is good enough or elect to embark on the somewhat more challenging task of shaping the cat to stand on its hind legs and walk.

Once the cat is sitting up, it may or may not spontaneously start to stand on its hind legs. Some cats do, but many don't. If the cat just sits there without starting to rise up on its hind legs, try to elicit standing by holding a treat above the cat's head. Then, as soon as the cat starts to rise, sound the clicker and give it the treat. On the next trial, wait a bit before again eliciting a stand by holding out a treat. If you are patient enough, the animal will eventually start to stand on its hind legs spontaneously. Finally, if you want the animal to walk on its hind legs, you will have to wait for or elicit behavioral variants in which the animal not only stands up on its hind legs but walks increasingly long distances before you sound the clicker and give it a treat.

If you decide to train your cat, you will discover that training a real animal is harder than training Sniffy. One reason for the difference is that your cat has a larger behavior repertoire than Sniffy, and another is that the cat is free to move about and approach you in a way that Sniffy cannot. One difficulty will almost certainly arise. During magazine training, when you start to move away from the cat, it will follow you. If you sit down with the treats and clicker in hand, the cat will jump into your lap. If you are standing up and walking, the cat may jump on your shoulder. When these problems arise, don't punish the cat. You will significantly retard the learning process if you do anything to frighten the animal. However, if you never give the cat a treat unless you have first sounded the clicker, and if you never sound the clicker unless the cat is on the floor, the cat will eventually learn to stay off you and "cooperate."

Clicker training is also a technique that has become popular with many dog trainers. However, because dogs form stronger social bonds with people than cats do, enthusiastic verbal praise and physical affection are often the only reinforcers that dogs require. For a dog, the verbal praise probably comes to act as a secondary reinforcer that predicts the availability of physical affection. Whether treats should ever be used in addition to physical affection is a somewhat controversial issue among dog trainers.

Another variant of operant conditioning that professional animal trainers use to teach animals to perform sequences of behaviors is called *backward chaining*. For example, suppose that you wanted to train a rat to climb a ladder, walk across an elevated plank to a door, and open the door to obtain food. You would first train the rat to go through the open door to the food, then you would shape it to open the door to get access to the food. The next step would be to place the rat on the elevated platform at the top of the ladder so that it has to "walk the plank" to get to the door. Finally, you would shape ladder climbing to get to the platform. In other words, the idea of backward chaining is first to train the animal to do the last thing in the sequence just before receiving the food. Then you make the opportunity to perform the last behavior in the sequence contingent on performing the next-to-last behavior, and so on. Most of the complex trained animal performances that you see in a circus or zoo are achieved through a combination of shaping and backward chaining.

Some Questions and Things to Do

To get additional information about how the principles of operant conditioning can be applied in the real world, search the World Wide Web for pages dealing with *clicker training*. You'll find numerous articles on how to train dogs, cats, horses, fish, and many other kinds of animals. Many people have a lot of fun training their animals to do a large variety interesting and useful things. You will also discover how operant conditioning is employed to modify human behavior. For example, some coaches use clicker training to improve the performances of athletes.

You can set up experiments on extinction, spontaneous recovery, secondary reinforcement, reinforcement scheduling, stimulus discrimination, and stimulus generalization using files in which Sniffy has been trained to beg, face wipe, or roll. The results of these explorations will be variable. In some instances, you will obtain results that parallel those obtained with bar pressing. In other cases, you will get quite different results.

Because the Sniffy Lite program always employs the same neural-network model of operant conditioning, you can be sure that the differences you observe are not due to differences in the underlying mechanisms of learning.[1] Instead, differences in things like scheduling effects and stimulus generalization must be the result of differences in the places the behaviors are performed and in the way the movements cause Sniffy to interact with his environment in the operant chamber.

Think about differences between bar pressing and the other behaviors that might account for any differences you observe:

- Bar pressing is the only behavior in Sniffy's repertoire that involves interaction with a device (the bar). What is the importance of that?
- Bar pressing is the only behavior that must be performed in close proximity to the hopper into which the magazine drops food pellets. Is that important?
- Bar pressing can be repeated rapidly. For which other behaviors is that true? What factors limit the frequency with which other behaviors can be performed?

---

[1] We know that Sniffy always employs the same learning mechanism because we didn't give him any others. Psychologists often assume that animals always employ the same learning mechanisms, but that assumption may not always be correct with live animals.

APPENDIX

How to Manage Your Sniffy Lite Files

Floppy Disks and Hard Disks

Floppy disks are small, portable devices that can hold small amounts of data. Each floppy disk is capable of storing about 1400 kilobytes (KB) of data. Here is a picture of a floppy disk of the kind used in many contemporary Windows computers and in older Macintosh computers.

In addition, your computer contains one or more hard disks. A **hard disk** is a device located inside your computer. The hard disks in contemporary computers usually have storage capacities ranging from as little as 800 megabytes (MB) up to 100 gigabytes (GB) of data. The fact that 1 MB = 1024 KB, and 1 GB = 1024 MB means that your computer's hard disk can store from several hundred to many thousands of times as much data as a floppy disk.

Sniffy Lite data files range in size from as little as 240 KB for the shortest, least complex exercises up to about 900 KB for the longest, most complex exercises. The point of all this arithmetic is to point out that although you cannot store very many Sniffy files on a floppy disk, you can store a very large number of Sniffy files on your computer's hard disk. It is for this reason that *we strongly urge you to save your Sniffy files on your computer's hard disk.*

In addition, Sniffy data files grow during experiments. A Sniffy file that occupies 250 KB of disk space when you save it immediately after setting up an experiment might require 900 KB of disk space when you save it again after the experiment has been completed. Sniffy files grow as experiments progress because the Sniffy Lite program records a lot of information about Sniffy's behavior and psychological processes during experiments. For this reason, if you saved a Sniffy file on a floppy disk, the floppy disk might have enough room to save the file at the beginning of the experiment but not at the end. In that event, you would get an error message when you tried to save the file on the floppy disk at the end of the experiment, and you might end up having to do the exercise over again. This is another reason why *we implore you to save your Sniffy files on your hard disk, not on a floppy disk.*

Here are some tips that will save time and minimize frustration:

- *Always save your Sniffy files on the hard disk of the computer you're using.*
- *If your professor wants you to hand in your Sniffy files on a floppy disk:*
  - Save the files on the hard disk of the computer that you're using when you create the files.
  - Then copy the files from the computer's hard disk onto one or more floppy disks and give them to your professor when the time comes to hand in the files. We explain in detail how to copy files onto floppy disks in a later section of this appendix.
  - A second advantage of this approach is that if you or your professor loses the floppy disk containing your files, you will still have a copy of the files on your computer's hard disk.
- *If you don't have your own computer and must store your Sniffy files on floppy disks:*
  - Save your Sniffy files on the hard disk of the computer that you're using when you create the files.
  - Copy your files from the hard disk onto one or more floppy disks when the experiment is completed.
  - Copy your files from your floppy disks back onto the hard disk of the computer that you're using before you use the files again.
  - Because floppy disks are fragile and easily damaged, always keep at least two copies of your files on different floppy disks.

Here are some tips to reduce the chance of losing data stored on floppy disks:

- Keep your floppy disks in a sturdy container designed for storing floppy disks.
- Never carry an unprotected floppy disk in your pocket or purse.
- Keep your floppy disks away from heat sources such as radiators or direct sunlight.
- Keep your floppy disks away from anything that contains a magnet. For example, don't set a floppy disk on top of a stereo speaker, which contains a magnet that could erase the data. Telephone handsets also contain magnets that might be a hazard to floppy disks.

Deciding Where to Save Your Files

In Windows, the Sniffy Lite installer places your files in a folder called Sniffy Lite for Windows, which is located inside a folder called Program Files on your C drive. The following picture shows a typical Windows XP installation. The open Sniffy Lite for Windows folder is displayed in front of the open Program Files folder.

To display the windows this way, you would do the following.

- To show the Program Files window:
  - Click with your left mouse button while pointing at the Start icon in the task bar at the bottom of your screen. In the pop-up menu that appears above the Start icon, select My Computer.
  - In the My Computer window, double-click with your left mouse button on the icon that appears under Hard Disk Drives.
  - In the Hard Disk window that appears, left double-click on the Program Files icon.
  - If all you wanted to see were the contents of the Sniffy Lite for Windows folder by itself, you could now simply left double-click on that folder's icon.

- To show both the Sniffy Lite for Windows window and the Program Files window simultaneously (as in the illustration):
  - □ Repeat the steps given above to show a second copy of the Program Files window.
  - □ Left double-click on the Sniffy Lite for Windows icon to display the Sniffy Lite for Windows window.
  - □ Rearrange and resize the windows to produce the display shown on the previous page.

The next picture shows a typical installation in Mac OS X. The installation instructions told you to place the Sniffy Lite program in your Applications folder. You were also instructed to create a folder called Sniffy Files inside your Documents folder and to place the Sample Files and other material inside it. In the illustration, we see parts of three windows: a portion of the "home" folder for a user named "adhb," a portion of a Documents folder containing a Sniffy Files folder, and a portion of a Sniffy Files folder showing several exercises and a Sample Files folder.

To display the windows in this fashion:

- Double-click the mouse button while pointing the cursor at the icon of the start-up disk. Unless you have moved it, the start-up disk icon will be always located in the upper right-hand corner of your desktop.

- With the Finder active, either choose the New Window command from the Window menu or press the N key while holding down the command key.
- In the new window that appears, click on the Documents icon in the panel on the left side of the window.
- Scroll through the Documents window to display the Sniffy Files folder.
- Repeat the previous two steps to display another copy of the Documents window and double-click on the Sniffy Files folder icon.
- Rearrange and resize the windows to display them as shown on the previous page.

To create a new folder in Windows:

- Point the cursor at the File menu located at the top of the folder's window and click your left mouse button.
- In the drop-down menu that appears, drag down to New, then drag across to Folder, and release the mouse button. A new folder appears.
- Immediately type the name that you want to give the new folder.

To create a new folder on a Macintosh:

- Click your mouse button once while pointing at the open folder window. (This operation ensures that the new folder will be created in the correct window.)
- Choose the New Folder command from the Finder's File menu. A new untitled folder appears.
- Immediately type the name you want to give the folder.

Getting Easy Access to the Sniffy Program and Files From Your Computer Desktop

Creating a Windows Shortcut

In Windows XP, the "ordinary" way of reaching your Sniffy Lite for Windows folder involves the following steps.

- Left click on the Start icon at the bottom of your screen.
- Select My Computer from the pop-up menu that appears above the Start icon.

- Open your hard drive root directory by left double-clicking on the icon below the words "Hard Disks."
- Left double-click on the Program Files icon.

What a process! Fortunately, there is a simple way to reduce the number of steps involved: Create a shortcut to your Sniffy Lite for Windows folder and place the shortcut on your Windows desktop. Here is what you need to do to set up the shortcut.

- Go through the four steps listed above to open your Program Files window.
- While pointing the cursor at the Sniffy Lite for Windows folder icon, click and hold down your right mouse button.
- A drop-down menu appears with a number of commands listed.
- Release the mouse button, drag the cursor down to the Create Shortcut command, and click on it with your left mouse button.
- A folder icon with an arrow on it titled Shortcut to Sniffy Lite for Windows appears inside your Program Files folder.
- Click on the shortcut icon with your left mouse button, hold the mouse button down, and drag the icon onto your Windows desktop.

Once the shortcut icon is on the desktop, you can drag it around and place it wherever you want it. In the future, all you have to do to open your Sniffy Lite for Windows folder is to left double-click the shortcut icon.

If you want, you can follow an analogous procedure to create and place on your desktop a shortcut to the Sniffy Lite program. A shortcut to the program can be left doubled-clicked to launch the program. Dragging the icon of a Sniffy Lite file onto the program shortcut will launch the program and open the file.

Placing Aliases in the Mac OS X Dock

For Mac OS X users, the easiest way of quickly launching the Sniffy Lite program and getting to your Sniffy Files folder is to place aliases of the program and the folder in the Mac OS X dock.

To place an alias of the program in the dock:

- Locate the Sniffy Lite for Macintosh program in your Applications folder.
- Click once on the program icon and, while holding the mouse button down, drag the program icon into the dock.

- If your dock is displayed horizontally at the bottom of your screen, drag the program icon to any convenient place left of the vertical line that separates program icons from folder icons.
- If your dock is displayed vertically on the left or right side of your screen, drag the program icon to any convenient place above the line that separates program icons from folder icons.

When the program icon is in the dock, you can launch the program by clicking once on the dock icon.

To place an alias of your Sniffy Files folder in the dock:

- Locate your Sniffy Files folder inside your Documents folder.
- Click once on the folder icon and, while holding the mouse button down, drag the folder icon into the dock.
- If your dock is displayed horizontally at the bottom of your screen, drag the folder icon to any convenient place to the right of the vertical line that separates program icons from folder icons.
- If your dock is displayed vertically on the left or right side of your screen, drag the folder icon to any convenient place below the line that separates program icons from folder icons.

When the Sniffy Files folder is in the dock, you can open the folder by clicking once on the folder icon in the dock. You can also launch the Sniffy Lite program and simultaneously open a particular file by dragging a Sniffy program file icon onto the program icon in the dock.

Saving Files

Let's imagine you have come to the point in the instructions for an exercise where we tell you to execute the Save As command and save the exercise with some specified name in an appropriate place on your computer's hard disk. Here is specific information about what Windows and Macintosh users need to do at that point in order to save the file in the place where we suggest that you keep your Sniffy Lite files.

Saving Files in Windows XP

We assume that you want to save a file in a folder called My Sniffy Files that is located inside the Sniffy Lite for Windows folder on your hard disk.

■ Select the Save As command from the File menu in the *Sniffy Lite* program. A dialog box resembling the following will appear.

Look carefully at the dialog box. At the top after the words "Save in:" is a space containing an icon and the name of the place where the file will be saved unless you do something to change the location. In this case, the icon is a picture of an open folder, which tells you the current place is a folder. Different icons would appear for different kinds of places (for example, the desktop, a floppy disk, or the root level of a hard disk[1]).

In the large white space below the place name is a closed folder icon with the name Sample Files and several file icons with their associated file names. This part of the dialog box always displays the contents of the place named in the area to the right of "Save in:". Depending on what's in the currently displayed location, you may see names and icons representing files, folders, hard disks, or a floppy disk.

If the name after "Save in:" is the place where you want to save your file, all you have to do is:

■ Type the name that you want to give the file in the text box located to the right of "File name:".

■ Point the cursor at the command button labeled Save and click once with your left mouse button.

[1] The root level of a hard disk is the contents you see when you open a hard-disk icon by double-clicking on it.

If the name to the right of "Save in:" is not the place where you want to save the file (for instance, if it's not your Sniffy Lite for Windows folder), clicking on the small triangle at the right side of the box where the current location is displayed will change the dialog box so that it resembles the following illustration.

The area inside the box below "Save in:" now shows a diagram of the relationships between your current location and other places where your computer might be able to save files. Remember that your Sniffy Lite for Windows folder is inside the Program Files folder which is inside the hard drive (C: drive). By left double-clicking on icons in the location diagram, you can navigate from wherever you happen to be until you find your Sniffy Lite for Windows folder. Once you reach the Sniffy Lite for Windows folder:

- Point the cursor at the text box to the right of "File name:" and click the left mouse button once.
- Type the name that you want to give the file.
- Point the cursor at the Save command button and click once with your left mouse button.

If you are using a version of Windows other than Windows XP, the dialog boxes may look somewhat different, but the principles involved in saving a file in a particular place will be very similar.

Saving Files in Mac OS X

We assume that you want to save a file in a folder called Sniffy Files that is located inside the Documents folder on your hard disk.

- Select the Save As command from the File menu in the Sniffy Lite program. Either an abbreviated or a detailed version of the Save dialog box may appear. The abbreviated version of the dialog box is shown below.

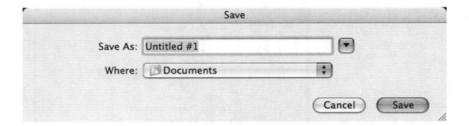

- If the abbreviated dialog box appears, click on the button with a triangle in it that is located on the right end of the text box next to "Save As:". Clicking on the triangle will cause the detailed version of the dialog box, shown below, to appear.

Look carefully at the detailed dialog box. At the top to the right of the words "Save As:" is a text box into which you will type the name that you want to give the file. Because in this instance the file has not yet been named, the name Untitled #1 appears.

Below the text box is a button showing a folder icon and the name of the location where the file will be saved unless you do something to change the location. In the example shown, the word Documents indicates that the file will be saved in your Documents folder unless you change the location.

The main part of the dialog box consists of two large white spaces separated by a vertical column. The area directly below the button containing the name of the current location contains a list of places in your user area of the computer. Note that the word "Documents" and the icon to its left are highlighted. The highlighting is another indication that the Documents folder is your current location.

The large white area to the right of the vertical bar displays the contents of the highlighted item in the left panel. In this instance, because the Documents folder is highlighted, the right panel displays the contents of the Documents folder.

We assume that you want to save the file in your Sniffy Files folder. To do so,

- Click once on the Sniffy Files folder in the right panel. Then the items that had been displayed in the right panel move into the left panel and the contents of the Sniffy Files folder is displayed in the right panel.
- Once you're in the place where you want to save your file:
  □ Type the name that you want to give the file in the text box under "Save As:".
  □ Point the cursor at the Save command button and click your mouse button once.

Opening Files

Opening Files in Windows XP

There are several ways to open files in Windows, but we will describe only the most basic approaches. In the first example, we assume that you have already started the Sniffy Lite program and that you have just executed the Open command found under the File menu. When you execute the Open command, the Sniffy Lite program will always put up a dialog box asking whether you want to save the file that is currently open. If you want to save the file, click on the Yes command button and go through the file-saving process. If you do not want to save the file (for example, because you've just started the Sniffy Lite program and there is no point in saving an Untitled file that contains no data), click the No command button. In either case, a dialog box resembling the following will appear.

In many ways, the Open dialog box resembles the Save dialog box. Here are the main things to note about it:

- At the top in the space to the right of "Look in:" is the name of the place (the folder or disk) whose contents are currently being shown.
- The icon just to the left of the place name tells you what kind of place it is. In the example, the open folder icon tells us that we are examining the contents of a folder.
- To the right of the place name is a button with a triangle on it. Clicking on this button will produce a box inside the dialog box showing the location of the current place in the hierarchy of folders and drives where there might be files that you could open. If you need to, you can scroll around to find the file you want.

- In the large area in the middle of the dialog box is a listing of the contents of the place named at the top. You will see the names of the various items with icons that identify what kinds of items they are.
- When you see the name of the file that you want to open, point the cursor at its icon and click your left mouse button once. The name of the file will appear in the text box located to the right of "File name:" at the bottom of the dialog box.
- When you've identified the right item, point the cursor at the Open command button and click your left mouse button once to open the file.

A second way to open a file in Windows is to open your Sniffy Lite for Windows and left double-click on the file icon.

- If the program is not running, it will start up automatically with the file you selected open.
- If the program is running, you will be asked whether you want to save the file that was already open before the file on which you just left double-clicked is opened.

A third way to open a file is to drag the file icon onto the icon of the program or onto the icon of a shortcut to the program.

- If the program is not running, it will start up automatically with the file you selected open.
- If the program is running, you will be asked whether you want to save the file that was already open before the file whose icon you just dragged is opened.

Opening Files in Mac OS X

There are several ways to open files on a Macintosh, but we will describe only the most basic approaches. In the first example, we assume that you have already started the Sniffy Lite program and that you have just executed the Open command found under the File menu. When you execute the Open command, the Sniffy Lite program will always put up a dialog box asking whether you want to save the file that is currently open. If you want to save the file, click on the Save command button and go through the file-saving process. If you do not want to save the file (for example, because you've just started the Sniffy Lite program and there is no point in saving an Untitled file that contains no data), click the Don't Save command button. In either case, a dialog box resembling the following will appear.

In many ways, this Open dialog box resembles the Save dialog box. Here are the main things to note about it:

- At the top is a button containing the name of the place (the folder or disk) whose contents are currently being shown.
- The icon just to the left of the place name tells you what kind of place it is. In the example, the folder icon tells us that we are examining the contents of a folder.
- Clicking on the place name button will produce a drop-down menu showing the location of the current place in the hierarchy of folders and disks where there might be files that you could open and a list of folders in which you have recently opened or saved files. If you are not in your Sniffy Files folder, you may see it in the list of recent places. If it's there, you can select it from the list.
- In the large area below the place name button are two panels separated by a vertical bar. The panel on the left contains the place named at the top of the dialog box. In the panel on the right is a list of the contents of that place. When you are inside the Sniffy Files folder, you will see a list of files and other items.
- Select the file that you want to open by clicking on it once.
- Then click on the Open command button at the bottom right of the dialog box.

A second way to open a file in Mac OS X is to open your Sniffy Files folder and double-click on a file icon.

- If the program is not running, it will start up automatically with the file you selected open.
- If the program is running, you will be asked whether you want to save the file that was already open before the file on which you just double-clicked is opened.

A third way to open a file is to drag the file icon onto the icon of the program or onto the icon of an alias to the program. This is an especially handy way of opening a file if you have aliases of the program and your Sniffy Files folder in the dock. Just click on the folder icon to open the folder. Then drag the icon of the file that you want to open onto the program icon in the dock.

- If the program is not running, it will start up automatically with the file you selected open.
- If the program is running, you will be asked whether you want to save the file that was already open before the file whose icon you just dragged is opened.

Copying Files From a Hard Disk to a Floppy Disk

Instructions for Windows XP Users

Many contemporary Windows computers have floppy disk drives. Add-on internal and external drives can also be purchased relatively inexpensively for computers that did not come with one already installed. To copy one or more files from your hard drive onto a floppy disk:

- Open your Sniffy Lite for Windows folder. If you made a shortcut to the folder and placed it on your desktop, left double-click on the shortcut icon. Otherwise:
  - ▢ Left click on the Start icon at the bottom of your screen.
  - ▢ In the pop-up menu that appears, select My Computer.
  - ▢ In the My Computer window, left double-click on the hard drive icon.
  - ▢ In the window that appears, left double-click on the Program Files folder.
  - ▢ In the Program Files window, left double-click on the Sniffy Lite for Windows folder.
- In the Sniffy Lite for Windows window, select the files that you want to copy to the floppy disk.

- Left click once on the Edit menu at the top of the Sniffy Lite for Windows folder.
- In the drop-down menu that appears, select Copy to Folder.
- In the dialog box that appears, select 3 1/2 Floppy (A:).
- Left click once on the Copy button at the bottom of the dialog box.
- Windows will present an animation telling you that it is copying the files.
- If there is not enough room on the floppy disk to hold all the files that you want to copy, Windows will put up a dialog box saying that the destination disk is full. If that happens:
    - Remove the full floppy disk from the floppy drive by pressing the button on the front of the drive.
    - Insert a new floppy.
    - Click on the Retry command button in the full-disk dialog box to continue copying on the new floppy disk.

Instructions for Mac OS X Users

Because Apple Computer, Inc., considers floppy disks to be an obsolete storage medium, new Macintosh computers have not contained floppy drives for the past several years. However, external add-on drives are available on the market; and Mac OS X handles the copying of files to and from floppy disks adequately.

- Plug your external floppy drive into a USB port on your computer.
- Insert a floppy disk in the drive.
- The floppy disk icon will appear on the right side of your desktop in the first available space under the icon for your startup disk.
- Open the folder in which you have stored your Sniffy files on your hard disk.
- Place the folder window in a position so that both the names of the files that you want to copy and the floppy disk icon are visible.
- Select one or more files that you want to copy.
- Point the cursor at one of the files, hold down the mouse button, and drag the files onto the floppy disk icon. When the icon darkens, release the mouse button. (As an alternative, you could open the floppy disk window and drag the files that you want to copy into the window.)
- The Macintosh operating system will present an animation telling you that it is copying the files.
- If there is not enough room on the floppy disk to hold all the files that you have selected, the operating system will tell you so. If that happens, select fewer files and try again.

- Dismount the floppy disk by dragging the disk icon into the trash.
- When the disk icon disappears, eject the floppy disk from the drive by pressing the button on the front of the drive.

Copying Files From a Floppy Disk to a Hard Disk

Instructions for Windows XP Users

This procedure is basically the mirror image of the procedure for copying files from your hard disk to a floppy disk.

- Place the floppy disk containing the files that you want to copy in your floppy disk drive.
- Click on the Start icon at the bottom of your screen.
- Select My Computer from the pop-up menu.
- Open the 3 1/2 Floppy [A:] window by left double-clicking on its icon.
- Open your Sniffy Lite for Windows window.
- Arrange the 3 1/2 Floppy [A:] window and Sniffy Lite for Windows window so that the names of the files you want to copy are visible. (If your desktop is crowded, only a small part of your Sniffy Lite for Windows window needs to be visible.)
- Use your left mouse button to select one or more files in the floppy disk window. You know when you have selected a file because it darkens.
- Point the cursor at one of the files, hold down the left mouse button, and drag the files into the Sniffy Lite for Windows folder window.
- Windows will present an animation telling you that it is copying the files.
- When the copying process is completed, remove the floppy disk from the floppy drive by pressing the button on the front of the drive.

Instructions for Mac OS X Users

This procedure is basically the mirror image of the procedure for copying files from your hard disk to a floppy disk.

- Connect your external floppy drive to a USB port on your computer.
- Place the floppy disk containing the files that you want to copy in your floppy disk drive.

- The floppy disk icon will appear on the right side of your desktop in the first available space under the icon for your startup disk.
- Open the folder into which you want to copy the files.
- Open the floppy disk window.
- Arrange the floppy disk window and the Sniffy Files window so that the names of the files you want to copy are visible. (If your desktop is crowded, only a small part of the Sniffy Files window needs to be visible.)
- Use your mouse button to select the files that you want to copy.
- Point the cursor at one of the files you want to copy, hold down the mouse button, drag the files into the destination window, and release the mouse button.
- The Macintosh operating system will present an animation telling you that it is copying the files.
- To dismount and eject a floppy disk from your floppy drive:
  - □ Select the floppy disk icon by clicking on it once. The icon will darken.
  - □ Wait a moment.
  - □ With the cursor pointed at the floppy disk icon, depress and hold down the mouse button, and drag the floppy disk icon to the trash can.
  - □ After the disk icon has disappeared, eject the disk from the drive by pressing the button on the front of the drive.

Using Sniffy Lite Macintosh Files on a Windows PC and Vice Versa

Sniffy Lite for Macintosh files are fully compatible with Sniffy Lite for Windows files, and vice versa. You can create a file on one kind of computer and look at the file on the other kind of computer. You can even set up an experiment on one kind of computer, save the file while the experiment is in progress, and then complete the experiment on the other kind of computer.

To transfer files from a Windows PC to a Macintosh:

- Copy the Sniffy Lite for Windows files onto a floppy disk.
- Insert the floppy disk into a Macintosh floppy disk drive. (Your Macintosh is capable of reading and writing 1.4 MB floppy disks that have been formatted on a PC.)
- When you open the floppy disk window, you will notice that all the Sniffy Lite for Windows file names end with the ".sdf" suffix. This

will be true even though the suffix is ordinarily invisible in Windows.

- Copy the Sniffy Lite for Windows files onto your Macintosh hard drive.
- Start your Sniffy Lite for Macintosh program.
- Use the Open command in the File menu to open the Sniffy Lite for Windows files.
- If you plan to use the files in Windows again, be sure to save each file with the ".sdf" suffix appended to each file name.

To transfer files from a Macintosh to a Windows PC:

- Save the files you want to transfer on the Macintosh hard disk with the ".sdf" suffix appended to each file name. To recognize them as Sniffy files, Sniffy Lite for Windows needs the suffix.
- Copy the Sniffy Lite for Macintosh files onto your PC-formatted floppy disk.[2]
- Copy the files from the floppy disk onto your Windows hard disk.
- Start your Sniffy Lite for Windows program.
- Use the Open command under the File menu to open the Macintosh files.

Storing Files on a CD

Virtually all contemporary computers contain a drive that is capable of reading CDs. In many computers, the CD drive is also capable of burning[3] files onto a blank CD. Windows XP, Mac OS X, and Mac OS 9 have rudimentary software for burning CDs as part of the operating system. In addition, many programs are available for both Macintosh and Windows computers for burning CDs. Many of these programs enable you to format the CD and control the burning process in more sophisticated ways than is possible if you use the CD-burning software built into the operating system.

Most CDs have a capacity of 670 MB of data, which is approximately 490 times as much data as a floppy disk can hold. For this reason, you can store many more Sniffy files on a CD than on a floppy disk. However, CDs have a major drawback. Unless you have special software

---

[2]Virtually all floppy disks on the market today have been preformatted for use in a PC.

[3]The verb "burn" is typically used to describe the action of writing files onto a blank CD.

that permits burning multiple sessions and a CD drive capable of writing to multiple-session CDs, burning files onto a CD is a one-time-only event. No new files can be added to a CD once a first batch of files have been burned onto it. Nevertheless, blank CDs have become so inexpensive that this problem isn't as serious as it sounds. Once data have been transferred from a CD to a computer's hard drive, you can probably afford to throw the CD away and use a fresh one when you want to store another batch of files.

Using CDs to transfer data from one computer to another offers a viable alternative to floppy disks, especially if you have a newer computer that did not come with a floppy disk drive. At some schools, students currently use CDs to hand in various kinds of files to professors. For example, if your professor asks you to perform several Sniffy experiments and use them as the basis for a paper, s/he might be willing to let you hand in everything (Sniffy files, data analysis files, and your paper) on a CD.

Because of the great variety of CD-burning software on the market, explaining the process of burning CDs is beyond the scope of this manual. You should consult the manual or Help files that came with your operating system or with the CD-burning software that you have installed on your computer to learn what you need to do.

E-mailing Files

Another good way to transfer files from one computer to another or to hand in files to your instructor is to include the files as e-mail attachments. Many students use e-mail to send pictures and other kinds of computer files to their friends. You can use the same process to transfer Sniffy files from one computer to another or to hand in files to your instructor. To transfer a file from your computer at home to a computer at school, either use your existing home and school e-mail accounts or get a free e-mail account with Microsoft Hotmail, Yahoo, or any of the other providers who offer e-mail accounts that can be accessed from any computer connected to the Internet.

- To transfer a file from your home computer to a computer at school, send the file as an enclosure (or attachment) in an e-mail to yourself, using an e-mail address that can be accessed from the school computer or any Web browser. Then open the e-mail and download the file using the computer at school.

- To hand in a file to your instructor, just send the file as an enclosure (or attachment) in an e-mail to the professor's e-mail address.
- Here are a couple of things to keep in mind:
  - ▢ Many e-mail servers limit the amount of data that can be transferred in an enclosure in any one e-mail message. A typical limit is about 1 or 2 MB. This means that you may need to send two or more different e-mail messages to transfer all of your data if you need to send more than one large Sniffy file.
  - ▢ The free e-mail accounts available from Hotmail, Yahoo, and similar sources provide only a limited amount of storage space. When you have downloaded files at the destination computer, you may want to delete the e-mail messages from your account.

Because there is a wide variety of e-mail programs that people use, detailed instructions for sending and receiving e-mail and sending files as enclosures are beyond the scope of this manual. Fortunately, so many students (and instructors) use e-mail on a daily basis that you very likely already know how to do it. If you need more help, ask your classmates or your instructor.

Glossary

Acquisition In classical conditioning, the development of a conditioned response as the consequence of pairing the conditioned and unconditioned stimuli. In operant conditioning, the increase in the frequency of an emitted behavior as the result of reinforcing occurrences of the behavior.

Action strength The part of Sniffy's operant conditioning algorithm, displayed in the Operant Associations mind window, that increases as a consequence of repeatedly reinforcing a particular movement.

Backward chaining An operant training procedure used to teach an animal to perform an improbable series of behaviors. The animal is first trained to perform the last behavior in the chain that would occur just before reinforcement at the end of the series. Then the next-to-last behavior in the chain is trained by making the opportunity to perform the last behavior contingent on the performance of the next-to-last behavior, and so on.

Bar–sound association The part of Sniffy's operant conditioning algorithm, displayed in the Operant Associations mind window, that develops when manipulation of the bar is repeatedly followed by reinforcement.

Begging An operantly shapeable behavior in which Sniffy faces the observer, lifts up his front paws, and moves his head up and down.

Behavioral repertoire A list and description of all the behavior patterns that an animal emits.

Classical conditioning The form of learning that occurs when two stimuli are repeatedly presented in a temporal series so that occurrences of the first stimulus predict occurrences of the second stimulus.

Clock time Time as measured in the real world.

Conditioned emotional response A form of classical conditioning in which a conditioned stimulus acquires the capacity to elicit freezing and other fear-related behaviors as the result of being paired with an aversive unconditioned stimulus.

Conditioned response (CR) In classical conditioning, the learned response to a conditioned stimulus that develops as the result of repeatedly presenting the conditioned stimulus shortly before presenting the unconditioned stimulus. In operant conditioning, an emitted behavior whose frequency has been increased as the result of repeatedly reinforcing the behavior.

Conditioned stimulus (CS) In classical conditioning, a stimulus that has the ability to acquire the capacity to elicit a conditioned response as the result of presenting the stimulus just before presentations of an unconditioned stimulus in a series of trials.

Conditioned suppression An alternative name for the conditioned emotional response.

CS response strength The part of Sniffy's classical conditioning algorithm, displayed in the CS Response Strength mind window, that predicts the strength of Sniffy's response to the conditioned stimulus the next time it is presented.

Elicited behavior A particular behavior that occurs as the direct result of presenting a particular stimulus.

Emitted behavior A behavior pattern that an animal performs "spontaneously" and for which no eliciting stimulus exists.

Extinction In classical conditioning, the diminution and eventual elimination of a previously conditioned response that occurs as the result of repeatedly presenting the conditioned stimulus without the unconditioned stimulus. In operant conditioning, the reduction in frequency of a previously conditioned response that occurs when the response is no longer reinforced.

Face wiping An operantly shapeable behavior in which Sniffy wipes one of his front paws repeatedly across an eye.

Fear The part of Sniffy's classical conditioning algorithm, exhibited in the Sensitivity & Fear mind window, that predicts the likelihood that Sniffy will exhibit freezing and other "fear-related" behaviors.

Fixed interval (FI) schedule A reinforcement schedule in which reinforcement of an operantly conditioned behavior is available only after a time period of a consistent duration has elapsed since the previous reinforcement.

Fixed ratio (FR) schedule A reinforcement schedule in which an operantly conditioned behavior is reinforced only after a specified number of unreinforced responses, which is always the same for each reinforcement, have been performed.

Interval schedule In operant conditioning, a schedule of reinforcement in which a response can be reinforced only after a period of time has elapsed since the previous reinforcement.

Magazine training The procedure by which the sound of the food dispenser in an operant chamber is turned into a secondary reinforcer by pairing the sound with the delivery of food pellets.

Mind window A feature of the Sniffy program that displays certain parameters of Sniffy's algorithms for classical and operant conditioning. The parameters displayed correspond to psychological processes that psychologists have proposed as explanations for aspects of classical and operant conditioning. The mind windows show how changes in Sniffy's "psychological processes" are related to changes in Sniffy's behavior.

Movement ratio The proportion of time during the presentation of a conditioned stimulus that Sniffy is displaying freezing and other fear-related behaviors.

Negative punisher A stimulus whose removal as the consequence of a behavior makes that behavior *less* likely to occur under similar circumstances in the future.

Negative reinforcer A stimulus whose removal as the consequence of a behavior makes that behavior *more* likely to occur under similar circumstances in the future.

Operant conditioning A learned change in the likelihood that an emitted behavior will occur again under similar circumstances in the future that occurs as the result of the events that follow occurrences of the behavior.

Orienting response (OR) The initial, unlearned response to a conditioned stimulus.

Pain sensitivity The parameter of Sniffy's classical conditioning algorithm, displayed in the Sensitivity & Fear mind window, that predicts the duration of Sniffy's unconditioned response to the shock US the next time the shock occurs.

Pavlovian conditioning Another name for classical conditioning.

Positive punisher A stimulus whose presentation as a consequence of a behavior makes that behavior *less* likely to occur under similar circumstances in the future.

Positive reinforcer A stimulus whose presentation as a consequence of a behavior makes that behavior *more* likely to occur under similar circumstances in the future.

Primary punisher A stimulus whose capacity to function as a punisher is not dependent on previous experience.

Primary reinforcer A stimulus whose capacity to function as a reinforcer is not dependent on previous experience.

Program time Time as measured internally by the Sniffy program. When Sniffy is visible, the relationship between program time and clock time depends on animation speed. When Sniffy is hidden to "accelerate time," program time runs much faster than clock time.

Punishment The operation of presenting a positive punisher or removing a negative punisher as a consequence of a behavior pattern, with the result that the punished behavior pattern becomes less likely to occur under similar circumstances in the future.

RAM   Random access memory, one of the electronic components of a computer that in part determines whether or how well the computer can run a program.

Ratio schedule   A reinforcement schedule in which reinforcement for a response becomes available only after a number of unreinforced responses have been completed.

Reinforcement   In operant conditioning, the operation of presenting a positive reinforcer or removing a negative reinforcer as the consequence of a behavior pattern, with the result that the reinforced behavior pattern becomes more likely to occur under similar circumstances in the future. In classical conditioning, the presentation of the unconditioned stimulus after an occurrence of the conditioned stimulus.

Reinforcement schedule   A rule that determines which instances of a response to reinforce.

Respondent conditioning   Another name for classical conditioning.

Response measure   Any measurement of the duration, frequency, magnitude, or probability of a behavior.

Rolling   An operantly shapeable behavior in which Sniffy turns somersaults.

Secondary punisher   A stimulus whose capacity to act as a punisher depends upon its prior association with a primary punisher.

Secondary reinforcer   A stimulus whose capacity to act as a reinforcer depends upon its prior association with a primary reinforcer.

Shaping   An operant training procedure in which the animal is trained to perform an improbable target behavior as the consequence of reinforcing a series of behaviors that resemble the target more and more closely.

Sound–food association   The part of Sniffy's operant conditioning algorithm, displayed in the Operant Associations mind window, that develops when the delivery of a food pellet follows his hearing the sound of the food dispenser mechanism.

Spontaneous recovery   The reappearance of a previously extinguished classically or operantly conditioned response that occurs when the animal is returned to the testing situation after spending time in another environment, such as its home cage.

Stage (of a classical conditioning experiment)   A group of trials that must be completed before the next stage can begin.

Suppression ratio   A response measure used to measure the conditioned emotional response. The suppression ratio is equal to the response rate during a CS presentation divided by the sum of the response rate during the CS plus the response rate during the period immediately preceding the CS.

Target behavior   The behavior that a trainer seeks to get an animal to perform at the end of shaping.

Unconditioned response (UR)   In classical conditioning, the response elicited by an unconditioned stimulus.

Unconditioned stimulus (US)   In classical conditioning, a stimulus that has the intrinsic capacity to elicit an obvious and easy-to-measure response. In a standard classical conditioning training trials, the US is presented after the CS.

Variable interval (VI) schedule   A reinforcement schedule in which the period of time after reinforcement during which further responding is not reinforced varies from reinforcement to reinforcement.

Variable ratio (VR) schedule   A reinforcement schedule in which the number of unreinforced responses required before another response is reinforced varies from reinforcement to reinforcement.

Yoked experimental design   An experimental setup in which one animal's responding determines a second animal's schedule of reinforcement.

References

Annau, Z., & Kamin, L. J. (1961). The conditioned emotional response as a function of intensity of the US. *Journal of Comparative and Physiological Psychology, 54,* 428–432.

Domjan, M. (1998). *The principles of learning and behavior* (4th ed.). Pacific Grove, CA: Brooks/Cole.

Domjan, M. (2003). *The principles of learning and behavior* (5th ed.). Belmont, CA: Wadsworth.

Estes, W. K., & Skinner, B. F. (1941). Some quantitative properties of anxiety. *Journal of Experimental Psychology, 29,* 390–400.

Ferster, C. B., & Skinner, B. F. (1957). *Schedules of reinforcement.* New York: Appleton-Century-Crofts.

Guthrie, E. R. (1960). *The psychology of learning* (rev. ed.). Gloucester, MA: Smith.

Hanson, H. M. (1959). Effects of discrimination training on stimulus generalization. *Journal of Experimental Psychology, 58,* 321–333.

Honig, W. K., Boneau, C. A., Burstein, K. R., & Pennypacker, H. S. (1963). Positive and negative generalization gradients obtained under equivalent training conditions. *Journal of Comparative and Physiological Psychology, 56,* 111–116.

Hull, C. L. (1943). *Principles of behavior.* New York: Appleton-Century-Crofts.

Hull, C. L. (1952). *A behavior system.* New Haven, CT: Yale University Press.

Imada, H., Yamazaki, A., & Morishita, M. (1981). The effects of signal intensity upon conditioned suppression: Effects upon responding during signals and intersignal intervals. *Animal Learning and Behavior, 9,* 269–274.

James, W. (1890). *Principles of psychology.* New York: Holt.

Jenkins, H. M., & Harrison, R. G. (1960). Effects of discrimination training on auditory generalization. *Journal of Experimental Psychology, 59,* 246–253.

Jenkins, H. M., & Harrison, R. G. (1962). Generalization of inhibition following auditory discrimination learning. *Journal of the Experimental Analysis of Behavior, 5,* 435–441.

Kamin, L. J. (1968). Attention-like processes in classical conditioning. In M. R. Jones (Ed.), *Miami Symposium on the Prediction of Behavior: Aversive stimulation.* Miami, FL: University of Miami Press.

Keller, F. S., & Schoenfeld, W. N. (1950). *Principles of psychology.* New York: Appleton-Century-Crofts.

Kimble, G. A. (1961). *Hilgard & Marquis' Conditioning and Learning* (2nd ed). New York: Appleton-Century-Crofts.

Mazur, J. E. (1998). *Learning and behavior* (4th ed). Upper Saddle River, NJ: Prentice Hall.

Pavlov, I. P. (1927). *Conditioned reflexes* (G. V. Anrep, Trans.). London: Oxford University Press.

Polenchar, B. E., Romano, A. G., Steinmetz, J. E., & Patterson, M. M. (1984). Effects of US parameters on classical conditioning of cat hindlimb flexion. *Animal Learning and Behavior, 12,* 69–72.

Rescorla, R. A. (1973). Second order conditioning: Implications for theories of learning. In E. J. McGuigan & D. B. Lumsden (Eds.), *Contemporary approaches to conditioning and learning.* New York: Wiley.

Rescorla, R. A., & Wagner, A. R. (1972). A theory of Pavlovian conditioning: Variations in the effectiveness of reinforcement and nonreinforcement. In A. H. Black & W. F. Prokasy (Eds.), *Classical conditioning II: Current research and theory* (pp. 64–99). New York: Appleton-Century-Crofts.

Reynolds, G. S. (1975). *A primer of operant conditioning.* Glenview, IL: Scott, Foresman.

Rizley, R. C., & Rescorla, R. A. (1972). Associations in second-order conditioning and sensory preconditioning. *Journal of Comparative and Physiological Psychology, 81,* 1–11.

Schwartz, B., & Reisberg, D. (1991). *Learning and memory.* New York: W. W. Norton.

Seligman, M. E. P. (1968). Chronic fear produced by unpredictable electric shock. *Journal of Comparative and Physiological Psychology, 66,* 402–411.

Seligman, M. E. P., Maier, S. F., & Solomon, R. L. (1971). Unpredictable and uncontrollable aversive events. In F. R. Bruch (Ed.), *Aversive conditioning and learning* (pp. 347–400). New York: Academic Press.

Shettleworth, S. J. (1975). Reinforcement and the organization of behavior in the golden hamster: Hunger, environment, and food reinforcement. *Journal of Experimental Psychology: Animal Behavior Processes, 1,* 56–87.

Skinner, B. F. (1930). On the conditions of elicitation of certain eating reflexes. *Proceedings of the National Academy of Science (Washington), 15,* 433–438.

Skinner, B. F. (1935). Two types of conditioned reflexes and a pseudo type. *Journal of General Psychology, 12,* 66–77.

Skinner, B. F. (1938). *The behavior of organisms.* New York: Appleton-Century-Crofts.

Skinner, B. F. (1953). *Science and human behavior.* New York: Macmillan.

Skinner, B. F. (1971). *Beyond freedom and dignity.* New York: Knopf.

Spence, K. W. (1937). The differential response in animals to stimuli varying within a single dimension. *Psychological Review, 44,* 430–444.

Tarpy, R. M. (1997). *Contemporary learning theory and research.* New York: McGraw-Hill.

Thorndike, E. L. (1898). Animal intelligence. An experimental study of associative processes in animals. *Psychological Monographs, 2*(8).

Tolman, E. C. (1932). *Purposive behavior in animals and men.* New York: Appleton-Century-Crofts.

Index

A

Accelerate Time (Isolate Sniffy) command, 27–29
acquisition
    of conditioned response, 30–35
    defined, 30, 124
action strength
    defined, 52–53, 124
    in extinction, 67
    in schedule of reinforcement, 80–83, 88
    in shaping, 56–57, 92, 94, 97
animation, of Sniffy, 2, 14

B

backward chaining, 101, 124
bar presses
    in extinction, 62–67
    interpreting cumulative records, 59–62
    measuring movement ratio, 12
    measuring suppression ratio, 12–13
    in operant chamber, 45
    shaping Sniffy for, 54–59
bar–sound association
    defined, 52, 124
    in extinction, 67
    in secondary reinforcement, 69
    in shaping, 56–57
beep sound, 29
begging, 91–93, 99–101, 124
behavioral repertoire, 49, 71–72, 124
brain, learning processes, 3–4

C

Cancel button, 17
cats, shaping behavior in, 99–101
CDs, 121–122

CER (conditioned emotional response)
    defined, 124
    Design Classical Conditioning Experiment
        dialog box, 14–17
    overview of, 11–14
classical conditioning, 7–40
    acquisition in, 10, 30–35
    background to, 10–11
    conditioned emotional response in, 11–14
    CS Response Strength mind window, 18–19
    cumulative records in, 20
    defined, 3, 124
    Design Classical Conditioning Experiment
        dialog box, 14–17
    exporting results, 23–24
    extinction in, 30
    getting reliable results, 21–22
    observations in, 22–23
    overview of, 19–20
    printing contents of data window, 24
    Sensitivity & Fear mind window, 17–18
    spontaneous recovery in, 30
    Suppression Ratio window, 21
    time acceleration, 28–30
Classical Conditioning Experiment Design dialog
        box
    measuring acquisition, 31–32
    measuring extinction, 35–36
    measuring spontaneous recovery, 37
    overview of, 14–17
clicker training, 99–101
clock time
    defined, 124
    program time vs., 13, 61

conditioned emotional response. *See* CER (conditioned emotional response)
conditioned punisher, 48
conditioned reinforcer, 48
conditioned response. *See* CR (conditioned response)
conditioned stimulus. *See* CS (conditioned stimulus)
conditioned suppression, 124. *See also* CER (conditioned emotional response)
continuous reinforcement, 63. *See also* CRF (continuous reinforcement) schedules
copying files, 117–120
Copy Window command, 25
covert behavior, 43
CR (conditioned response)
    in acquisition, 30–35
    in CS Response Strength mind window, 18–19
    defined, 10, 124
    in extinction, 30, 35–37
    in spontaneous recovery, 30, 37–39
CRF (continuous reinforcement) schedules
    defined, 57
    overview of, 73–75
    setting up, 80
CS (conditioned stimulus)
    in acquisition, 30–35
    in conditioned emotional responses, 11–14
    in cumulative records, 20
    defined, 124
    in Design Classical Conditioning Experiment dialog box, 16–17
    in extinction, 35–37
    overview of, 10
    reliability of results, 21–22
    in spontaneous recovery, 37–38
    in Suppression Ratio Window, 21
CS response strength, 124
CS Response Strength mind window
    exporting results, 23–24
    measuring acquisition, 32
    measuring extinction, 36–37
    measuring psychological states, 22
    measuring spontaneous recovery, 37
    overview of, 18–19
cumulative records, 20, 59–62

D

Delete Stage command, 16
Design Classical Conditioning Experiment command, 9, 14–15, 17, 31, 35, 37

Design Operant Conditioning Experiment dialog box, 58–59, 79–81
desktop shortcut, for Sniffy, 107–109
dock, in Mac OS X, 108–109
Don't Save command button, 115

E

elicited behavior, 45, 124
e-mailing files, 122–123
emitted behavior, 43–45, 125
environmental effects, 43–44
ethics, in use of live animals, 2
Export Data command, 23–24
extinction
    defined, 30, 125
    measuring, 35–37
    overview of, 62–67
    partial reinforcement and, 86–88
    secondary reinforcement and, 67–69
    spontaneous recovery and, 69–70
extinction burst, 64, 66

F

face wiping, 90, 93–95, 125
fear
    in acquisition, 33–34
    in CER, 11–14
    defined, 125
    in Sensitivity & Fear mind window, 17–18, 22, 33–34
FI (fixed-interval) schedules
    defined, 76, 125
    exercise, 84–85
    performance in, 78–79
file management, 103–123
    CD storage, 121–122
    copying and pasting visible windows, 24–25
    copying files, 117–120
    creating desktop access, 107–109
    e-mailing files, 122–123
    floppy disks vs.hard disks, 103–104
    Macintosh files in Windows and vice versa, 120–121
    opening, 113–117
    printing contents of data window, 24
    saving, 27–28, 31, 105–107, 109–113
FI scallop, 79
fixed-interval schedules. *See* FI (fixed-interval) schedules
fixed-ratio schedules. *See* FR (fixed-ratio) schedules

floppy disks
    copying files to and from, 117–120
    defined, 103
    saving files to, 27, 103–104
folders. *See* file management
food reinforcement
    in extinction. *See* extinction
    in magazine training, 51–54
    measuring suppression ratio, 12
    in operant chamber, 45–46
    in secondary reinforcement, 67–69
    Sniffy vs. real rat, 5
freezing, 11–14
FR (fixed-ratio) schedules
    defined, 75, 125
    exercise, 84–85
    performance in, 78
frustration, 66

H

hard disks
    copying files to and from, 117–120
    defined, 103
    saving files to, 27–28, 103–104

I

instrumental conditioning. *See* operant
    conditioning
Interval Between Trials text box, 16, 35
interval schedules, 76, 88, 125. *See also* FI (fixed-
    interval) schedules; VI (variable-interval)
    schedules
Isolate Sniffy (Accelerate Time) command, 27–29

L

Lab Assistant window, 9, 29
law of effect, 41–42
learning processes, 3–5

M

Mac OS X
    creating new folders, 107
    CS Response Strength window in, 32
    Design Classical Conditioning Experiment
        dialog box in, 14
    opening files, 115–117
    placing Sniffy Lite alias in dock, 108–109
    saving files, 106–107, 112–113
    starting Sniffy Lite, 7–10
    transferring files to Windows PC, 121

magazine, 42
magazine training
    accelerating with shaping, 55–59
    defined, 52, 125
    during extinction, 67–69
    overview of, 53–54
    self-training and, 72
    shaping behavior in cats, 99
Microsoft Windows XP
    creating new folders, 107
    CS Response Strength window in, 32
    Design Classical Conditioning Experiment
        dialog box in, 14
    desktop shortcut for Sniffy Lite, 107–108
    opening files, 113–115
    saving files, 105–106, 109–111
    starting Sniffy Lite, 7–10
    transferring files to Macintosh, 120–121
mind windows
    CS Response Strength, 18–19
    defined, 125
    Operant Associations, 52–53, 59, 81, 83
    overview of, 3–4
    Sensitivity & Fear, 17–18
movement ratio
    defined, 125
    measuring basic acquisition of CR, 30–35
    overview of, 12
    reliability of results, 21–22
Movement Ratio window
    in acquisition, 32
    exporting results, 23–24
    in extinction, 36
    overview of, 19–20
    in spontaneous recovery, 37
Mute Pellet Dispenser command, 68

N

negative punisher, 48, 125
negative reinforcer, 47, 125
neurophysiological learning processes, 3–4
New Stage command, 16, 35
Next Stage command, 16
Number of Trials text box, 16, 35

O

Open command, 67, 83, 113–114, 116
opening files
    in Mac OS X, 115–117
    in Windows XP, 113–115

Operant Associations mind window
    in cumulative records, 58
    in extinction, 66
    in magazine training, 53–54, 72
    overview of, 52–53
    in reinforcement schedules, 81, 83, 87
    in shaping, 56–58, 92–95, 97
operant chamber
    costs of, 1
    overview of, 45–46
    in work of B. F. Skinner, 42
Operant Chamber window, 9
operant conditioning, 41–72
    behavioral repertoire, 71–72
    B. F. Skinner and, 42–45
    CER using, 12
    cumulative records, 59–62
    defined, 3, 125
    Edward Thorndike and, 41–42
    extinction, 62–67
    magazine training, 53–54, 72
    Operant Associations mind window, 52–53
    operant chamber in, 45–46
    reinforcement and punishment, 46–49
    reinforcement schedules. *See* reinforcement
        schedule
    secondary reinforcement, 67–69
    shaping Sniffy to press bar with, 54–59
    spontaneous recovery, 69
    technique, 51–52
OR (orienting response), 10, 125

P

pain sensitivity
    defined, 125
    in Sensitivity & Fear mind window, 17–18, 22,
        33–34
partial reinforcement (PRF), 73–75, 86–87
Paste command, 25
Pavlovian conditioning, 10–11, 125
positive punisher, 47, 125
positive reinforcer, 47, 125
Previous Stage command, 15
PRF (partial reinforcement), 73–75, 86–87
primary punisher, 125
primary reinforcer, 125
Principles of Psychology (Thorndike), 41
Print Window command, 24
program time
    clock time vs., 13, 61
    defined, 125

psychological processes
    in classical conditioning, 33–34
    learning and, 3–5
    in work of B. F. Skinner, 44–45
punishment
    defined, 125–126
    in operant conditioning, 47–49
puzzle boxes, 41, 42

R

RAM (random access memory), 29–30, 126
ratio schedules, 75, 86–88, 126. *See also* FR
        (fixed-ratio) schedules; VR (variable-ratio)
        schedules
real animals
    CER conditioning with, 13
    frustration in, 66
    learning processes in, 3–5
    measuring acquisition with, 33
    in operant chamber, 46
    reinforcement schedules with, 85–86
    shaping behavior in, 89–90
    Sniffy Lite vs., 1–2, 4–5
regulations, animal-care, 1
reinforcement. *See also* magazine training;
        shaping
    defined, 126
    effect on extinction of partial, 86–88
    extinction of, 63–67
    negative, 47, 125
    in operant chamber, 45–46
    in operant conditioning, 46–49, 51–52
    partial, 73–75, 86–87
    positive, 47, 125
    secondary, 48, 52–53, 67–69, 126
    trouble when shaping behavior, 58
Reinforcement Action menu, 58
reinforcement schedule, 73–88
    defined, 73, 126
    fixed-interval, 78–79, 85
    fixed-ratio, 78, 84–85
    overview of, 73–76
    realism of Sniffy's performance, 85–86
    setting up Design Operant Condition Experi-
        ment dialog box, 79–81
    variable-interval, 77–78, 84
    variable-ratio, 77–78, 81–84
reinforcer, 47
Remove Sniffy for Time Out command, 37
respondent conditioning, 126. *See also* classical
        conditioning

response class, 55
response measures
    during classical conditioning, 23
    defined, 126
    Sniffy's probalistic behavior and, 34–35
rolling, 90, 95–98, 126
Run Classical Conditioning Experiment command,
    17, 31, 36, 37

S

satiation, 4
saving files
    on hard disk, 103–104
    location for, 105–107
    in Mac OS X, 112–113
    overview of, 105–107
    when opening files, 114
    in Windows XP, 109–111
schedule of reinforcement. *See* reinforcement
    schedule
Schedules of Reinforcement (Ferster and Skinner),
    75
secondary punisher, 48, 126
secondary reinforcers
    defined, 48, 126
    magazine training as, 52–53
    overview of, 67–69
Sensitivity & Fear mind window
    in acquisition, 33–34
    overview of, 17–18
    psychological states measured in, 22
shaping
    behaviors other than bar pressing, 89–91
    cats to beg or walk on hind legs, 99–101
    defined, 126
    Sniffy for bar presses, 54–59
    Sniffy to beg, 91–93
    Sniffy to roll, 95–98
    Sniffy to sniff, 98
    Sniffy to wipe face, 93–95
shaping hierarchy, 89
Shaping Tutor, 58–59
Show Sniffy command, 29
Skinner, B. F., 42–45, 59–60
sniffing, 98
Sniffy Files folder, 27–28
Sniffy Lite for Windows folder, 106–107
Sniffy Lite, overview of, 1–6
    about the program, 2–4
    creating animated Sniffy, 2
    as learning vs. research tool, 4–5

real-world applications of, 5–6
    reasons for creating, 1–2
    starting, 7–10
sound–food association
    defined, 52, 126
    in extinction, 67
    in secondary reinforcement, 69
    in shaping, 58
spontaneous recovery, 30, 37–38, 69, 126
stages, in classical conditioning
    defined, 126
    in extinction, 35–36
    overview of, 15–16
    in spontaneous recovery, 37
standards, animal-care, 1
stimulus
    in classical conditioning, 10
    conditioned. *See* CS (conditioned stimulus)
    in operant conditioning, 45–49
    Sniffy vs. real rat, 5–6
    unconditioned. *See* US (unconditioned
        stimulus)
suppression ratio
    in acquisition of CR, 30–35
    in CER, 12–13
    defined, 126
    reliability of results, 21–22
Suppression Ratio window
    in acquisition, 33
    exporting results, 23–24
    in extinction, 37
    overview of, 21
    in spontaneous recovery, 37–38

T

target behavior, 55, 126
Thorndike, Edward, 41–42
time acceleration, 28–30
trials, 42

U

unconditioned response (UR), 10, 126
unconditioned stimulus. *See* US (unconditioned
    stimulus)
UR (unconditioned response), 10, 126
US (unconditioned stimulus)
    in acquisition, 30–35
    CER using, 11–14
    in CS Response Strength mind window, 18
    cumulative records during, 20
    defined, 10, 126

US (unconditioned stimulus) *(continued)*
  measuring pain sensitivity, 18
  understanding results, 22

V

variable-interval schedules. *See* VI (variable-
    interval) schedules
variable-ratio schedules. *See* VR (variable-ratio)
    schedules
VI (variable-interval) schedules
  defined, 76, 126
  exercise, 84
  yoked experimental design and, 77–78

VR (variable-ratio) schedules
  in acquisition, 31
  defined, 75–76, 126
  exercises, 81–84
  reliability of results, 22
  in spontaneous recovery, 38–39
  yoked experimental design and, 77–78

W

Windows. *See* Microsoft Windows XP

Y

yoked experimental design, 77, 126

TO THE OWNER OF THIS BOOK:

I hope that you have found *Sniffy™, the Virtual Rat, LITE Version 2.0*, useful. So that this book can be improved in a future edition, would you take the time to complete this sheet and return it? Thank you.

School and address:_____

Department:_____

Instructor's name:_____

1. What I like most about this book is:_____

_____

_____

2. What I like least about this book is:

_____

_____

3. My general reaction to this book is:

_____

_____

4. The name of the course in which I used this book is:

_____

5. Were all of the chapters of the book assigned for you to read?_____

   If not, which ones weren't?_____

6. In the space below, or on a separate sheet of paper, please write specific suggestions for improving this book and anything else you'd care to share about your experience in using this book.

_____

_____

_____

WADSWORTH
CENGAGE Learning™

BUSINESS REPLY MAIL
FIRST-CLASS MAIL   PERMIT NO. 34   BELMONT CA

POSTAGE WILL BE PAID BY ADDRESSEE

Attn: **Psychology Editor**
Wadsworth
10 Davis Drive
Belmont, CA 94002-3098

FOLD HERE

OPTIONAL:

Your name:_____ Date: _____

May we quote you, either in promotion for *Sniffy™, the Virtual Rat, LITE Version 2.0,*
or in future publishing ventures?

Yes: _____ No: _____

Sincerely yours,

Tom Alloway
Greg Wilson
Jeff Graham